D1563722

John Ralston Saul's most recent book, *On Equilibrium,* was an immediate national bestseller on its publication in December 2001. Mr. Saul's philosophical trilogy — *Voltaire's Bastards, The Doubter's Companion* and *The Unconscious Civilization* — has had a growing impact on political thought in many countries. He is also the author of several novels of contemporary political and moral intrigue, which, like his non-fiction, have been translated into many languages.

Alain Dubuc is the president and editor of the daily newspaper *Le Soleil.* Under his leadership, the pages of *Le Soleil* have become a must-read for those concerned with the interplay of economics, ideas and politics in Quebec. Previous to running *Le Soleil,* Mr. Dubuc served as the éditorialiste en chef at *La Presse* in Montreal, where his own writings won the National Newspaper Award for Editorial Commentary in 2000.

 Georges Erasmus has made a lifelong contribution to the welfare and community of Canada's Aboriginal peoples. From 1976 to 1983 he served as the president of the Indian Brotherhood of the Northwest Territories / Dene Nation. He was subsequently elected as national chief of the Assembly of First Nations for two consecutive terms. In 1996 he co-chaired the groundbreaking Royal Commission on Aboriginal Peoples. He currently leads the Aboriginal Healing Foundation as president and chairman.

The LaFontaine-Baldwin Lectures
VOLUME ONE

A Dialogue on Democracy in Canada

John Ralston Saul,
Alain Dubuc AND
Georges Erasmus

EDITED BY

Rudyard Griffiths
OF THE DOMINION INSTITUTE

PENGUIN
CANADA

PENGUIN CANADA

Published by the Penguin Group

Penguin Books, a division of Pearson Canada, 10 Alcorn Avenue, Toronto, Ontario,
    Canada M4V 3B2

Penguin Books Ltd, 80 Strand, London WC2R ORL, England

Penguin Putnam Inc., 375 Hudson Street, New York, New York 10014, U.S.A.

Penguin Books Australia Ltd, 250 Camberwell Road, Camberwell, Victoria 3124,
    Australia

Penguin Books India (P) Ltd, 11, Community Centre, Panchsheel Park,
    New Delhi – 110 017, India

Penguin Books (NZ) Ltd, cnr Rosedale and Airborne Roads, Albany, Auckland 1310,
    New Zealand

Penguin Books (South Africa) (Pty) Ltd, 24 Sturdee Avenue, Rosebank 2196,
    South Africa

Penguin Books Ltd, Registered Offices: 80 Strand, London WC2R ORL, England

First published 2002

10 9 8 7 6 5 4 3 2 1

Author representation: Westwood Creative Artists
94 Harbord Street, Toronto, Ontario M5S 1G6

Manufactured in Canada.

NATIONAL LIBRARY OF CANADA CATALOGUING IN PUBLICATION DATA

Saul, John Ralston, 1947–
    The LaFontaine-Baldwin lectures : a dialogue on democracy in Canada /
John Ralston Saul, Alain Dubuc and Georges Erasmus ; edited by Rudyard Griffiths.

ISBN 0-14-301218-5

1. Representative government and representation—Canada.
2. Nationalism—Canada. 3. Native peoples—Canada. 4. Canada—Politics and
government—1993– I. Dubuc, Alain II. Erasmus, Georges III. Griffiths, Rudyard
IV. Title.

FC60.S36 2002   971.064'8   C2002-902397-1
F1008.3.S28 2002

Visit Penguin Books' website at **www.penguin.ca**

To Louis-Hippolyte LaFontaine and Robert Baldwin, two architects of Canadian democracy

∼ Contents

⁓ Acknowledgements

This book, and the creation of the LaFontaine-Baldwin Lectures, would not have been possible without the support of an outstanding group of public-minded individuals and organizations. The Dominion Institute and John Ralston Saul would like to thank TD Bank Financial Group for its generous multi-year support of the lecture series; Cynthia Good and Michael Schellenberg of Penguin Canada; Michael A. Levine, counsel to the lecture series; Richard Addis, former editor of the *Globe and Mail;* André Pratte and Caroline Jamet of *La Presse;* Bernie Lucht and Janice Ward of the Canadian Broadcasting Corporation; and the entire LaFontaine-Baldwin Advisory Board, for their continuing support.

∼ Introduction

When Canadians think about the founding of our democracy, we usually conjure up the textbook image of Confederation: men in waistcoats poring over mounds of parchment in high-windowed rooms. Beneath this benign pictogram lies a pernicious myth.

We have come to believe that the creation of our democratic values and institutions was a purely pragmatic exercise, a series of jurisdictional horse trades between

French and English Canada, between Mother England and its colonies. The birth of Canadian democracy, or so the story goes, was not the result of bold vision or charismatic leadership. Rather, the coming of democracy to the Canadas was supposedly the by-product of colonial elites' pursuit of economic gain and personal ambition through political union.

The convention that political expediency and self-interest defined Canada's journey from colonial oligarchy to democratic community does a great disservice to our public memory and present-day civic discourse.

At one moment, the belief that our democracy sprang from an act of political pragmatism erases the fact that our democratic culture was the product of profound choices among competing visions of the public good. Far more violent and intolerant futures than the present we inhabit could have flowed out of Canada's political founding. This inclination to see the coming of democracy to Canada as an inevitable and non-ideological process also devalues our present-day attitudes about civil society. It leads us to assume that our democratic culture is somehow an imperfect copy of the ideas and institutions that sprang from the great political experiment in America.

However, there is a different way to think about the origins of our democratic culture, one that gives us a deep appreciation of the political dynamism and intellectual originality of our democracy. This interpretation traces the genesis of Canadian democracy back to the rough-and-tumble decade of the 1840s and the actions and ideas of two great but largely forgotten heroes: Louis-Hippolyte LaFontaine and Robert Baldwin.

LaFontaine and Baldwin were political reformers whose lives were defined by the Rebellions of 1837. Both men believed passionately in the idea of responsible government — the principle that Canadians should be governed by a cabinet responsible to the elected legislature and not the executive fiat of the governor general. For Louis LaFontaine, the survival of French culture and the cause of liberty meant travelling to Britain to plead for reform, only to be imprisoned on his return to Quebec. Robert Baldwin, a prominent reform figure in pre-Rebellion administrations and the fountainhead of responsible government, condemned the armed insurrection in Upper Canada, but, in the Rebellion's aftermath, he found himself a social outcast, half a lifetime's thinking about political reform discredited by his peers.

Yet just ten years later, LaFontaine and Baldwin would lead Canada's first democratic government. As collaborators, they would give life to many of the institutions and values that we now associate with the democratic character of Canadian society. In the space of a decade they would also create a new political culture for Canada, one capable of subsuming divisions of language, ethnicity and religion in an overarching notion of the public good.

The genius of LaFontaine and Baldwin was the consistently principled, inclusive and democratic stance they took towards the series of social and political crises that defined the 1840s. In the wake of the 1837 Rebellions, the reform movement and French Canada were faced with the fallout from Lord Durham's disastrous 1837 report. On Durham's recommendation, the British Colonial Office had merged Upper and Lower Canada into one political unit represented by a single Parliament. The Colonial Office's long-term goal was the gradual assimilation of French-Canadian culture by the English-speaking majority. The immediate political intent of union was the dilution of the reform elements in both provinces in Parliament where the Protestant English minority in Quebec would combine with the Tory element in Upper Canada to form a powerful conservative majority.

As the 1840s got underway, the use of the French language was banned in the new legislature. During the elections for the first Parliament, the governor general aided and abetted sectarian violence against French and Anglo reformers. Wholesale political patronage was used to entrench Tory opponents of responsible government in key administrative positions. Democratic reform seemed an all but impossible goal.

What was the reaction of LaFontaine and Baldwin to these reversals, which followed so quickly on the humiliations of 1837? Both understood that the path to democracy lay in a policy of active collaboration between French and Anglo reformers. This collaboration would not consist of a return to rebellion. Rather, they would exploit the democratic potential of the new assembly to form a powerful French-Anglo reform majority. By winning legitimacy in the eyes of the public, this reform majority could wrestle executive authority over domestic affairs from the governor general.

Baldwin quickly put the reform agenda into action with two bold steps. First, he resigned from the Executive Council on the principle of responsibility when the governor general failed to heed his advice that reformers, including LaFontaine, be brought into the new administration. Next, he arranged for LaFontaine to run in a by-election in one of the two Toronto-area ridings that had elected Baldwin himself to Parliament. After losing his own seat to sectarian thuggery in Lower Canada, the leader of French Canada was triumphantly returned to Parliament by a Protestant, Upper Canadian constituency. This gesture cemented the French-Anglo reform partnership for the decade to come. It would also echo through the course of Canadian history, from the famous Macdonald-Cartier alliance all the way to the 1963 Royal Commission on Bilingualism and Biculturalism.

The hands-on task of bringing about responsible government fell to LaFontaine. Ever the brilliant parliamentary tactician, he used Baldwin's theories of responsible government to fight a protracted and public battle against the executive authority of the governors general. But his real contribution to Canadian democracy was in neutralizing the secessionist movement in Quebec, which saw co-operation with the Anglo reformers as a threat to the survival of French culture. Again and again, LaFontaine held together the French reform coalition against a radical republican movement, which sought political autonomy through annexation to the United States or outright revolt. Had LaFontaine lost his reform majority in and outside Parliament, the reform movement would have been stillborn in Upper Canada and Quebec set on the course to a second civil insurrection.

Democracy finally came to the Province of Canada in the winter of 1848. A landside election victory for

French and Anglo reformers and the arrival of a new liberal governor general made responsible government a fait accompli. It became fact when LaFontaine and Baldwin were called upon to form a new Executive Council and draw, as they saw fit, from the ranks of their reform party. LaFontaine and Baldwin were no doubt pleased that victory had been won not by adopting their opponents' tactics of gerrymandering and intimidation but by winning broad public support for the reform project and its vision of a shared democratic future for French and Anglo Canada. In ten short years, majority attitudes in the Province had undergone a seismic shift.

Of the reforms put into effect under the "Great Reform Ministry," three initiatives underline the vision of LaFontaine and Baldwin for a common democratic future that endures to present day. The use of French in the legislature and for government business was championed. Government was brought closer to the people through the establishment of locally elected, self-governing municipal councils. And the multi-decade fight over the relationship of organized religion to higher education was brought to an end with the creation of the University of Toronto as a publicly funded, non-sectarian institution.

The responsible government of Baldwin and LaFontaine faced its greatest test when it dealt with the

destruction of property that had occurred during the
rebellions. In the aftermath of the uprisings, the new
legislature approved equivalent indemnities for Upper
and Lower Canada. Yet it later became apparent that the
damages in Lower Canada were twice as great. To nail the
lid tight on the last major issue fuelling separatism there,
LaFontaine felt bound to pass legislation providing
adequate compensation for French Canadians. In doing
so, he tapped into long-standing Tory anger towards the
rebels and rekindled their fears, especially in Montreal,
about what the French reform majority would do with its
new-found power. In the midst of riot and bedlam in
Parliament and in the streets of Montreal, the governor
general held to the principle of responsible government
and made the bill law. That night, the Parliament of the
Province of Canada was burned to the ground by an
angry Tory mob.

In the aftermath of the burning of Parliament, the
democratic culture fostered by LaFontaine and Baldwin
triumphed. Rather than sending troops against the
rioters or executing their ringleaders — as was happening
all over Europe as the revolutions of 1848 were violently
suppressed — elite and public opinion rallied around the
reform values of political accommodation and social
tolerance. And in the absence of a martial response, the

spectre of the Rebellions that haunted French and Anglo relations was exorcised. It was almost as if the anger that had rotted at the core of both communities since 1837 was itself consumed in the blaze of Parliament.

The story of LaFontaine and Baldwin and their fight for responsible government opens up a whole new way of looking at the achievement of democracy in Canada. Instead of economic pragmatism or personal ambition, Canadian democracy flowed out of the political imagination and ethical force of LaFontaine and Baldwin's reform movement. The two men created the foundations for a democratic, egalitarian society where citizens could participate fully regardless of language or creed.

Their real genius, though, was to be able to imagine, in the dark days of the early 1840s, an inclusive and democratic future for Canada, and then lead a Province rife with sectarian division to this collective goal. Their patient adherence to an ethic of accommodation over withdrawal — their invention of a true politics of inclusion — saved their generation from the sectionalism that leads all too often to civil war. LaFontaine and Baldwin ultimately gave Canadians a distinct theory and style for the practice of democracy, one that has allowed us over 150 years to embrace successive waves of economic, demographic and technological change.

Discovering what is unique in the Canadian democratic experience and re-imagining a common democratic future for Canada are the twin goals of the LaFontaine-Baldwin Lecture series. Established by His Excellency John Ralston Saul in 2000, the annual LaFontaine-Baldwin lecture has quickly evolved into the pre-eminent national forum for exploring the historical antecedents and future trajectory of our democracy.

This volume contains the first three years of LaFontaine and Baldwin Lectures by John Ralston Saul, Alain Dubuc and Georges Erasmus. Each lecture stands by itself as a cogent analysis of the challenges and opportunities associated with the practice of democracy in Canada today. Together, they provide a powerful triangular framework — a fusion of the Anglo, French and Aboriginal perspectives — that propels us beyond the confines of our time and place to imagine, in the spirit of LaFontaine and Baldwin, the kind of democracy we think fairness and justice demands.

Rudyard Griffiths, Editor
September 2002

The
LaFontaine-Baldwin Lectures

VOLUME ONE

His Excellency John Ralston Saul

~ Inaugural LaFontaine-Baldwin Lecture

Royal Ontario Museum
Toronto, Ontario
Thursday, March 23, 2000

Why devote so much effort to the past, when tonight, in this city, there are four to five thousand homeless, a thousand of them children, half of them families with children?

Perhaps the answer lies in our reaction to these numbers: a little shudder of horror or surprise and then they roll off our back. The next time we hear them, well, we've already heard them. What else is new? And they remain, stubbornly, numbers, not people with lives.

So I add, what is the past when set against the thirty thousand who will experience homelessness over the next twelve months in Toronto, remembering that only 17 percent of them are chronically homeless? The vast majority, therefore, are caught on the precarious ledge of poverty for dozens of reasons, and from time to time are shoved off or slip off and then desperately crawl back up again. How many are on the ledge? Some eighty thousand in this city.

Do you feel those numbers intruding on you, crashing up against your sense of well-being and then rolling off, down to the floor? Tomorrow there will be more numbers from different sources on different subjects — an export number up or down; a dollar number up or down; inflation, unemployment, waiting times in emergency wards, a tax statistic, a student-debt calculation. Each will cause a sensation, positive, negative, a small catharsis, of the headline or police-drama sort.

These numbers have become our modern form of gossip; they are the *People* magazine of public policy.

Somehow, the lives that lie behind the drama cannot be integrated into our consciousness in a long-term way. Instead there is a sense of immobility. "That's the way things are." "There isn't the money." It is as if, seen from within the complexity of our systems, it is impossible to identify the relationship between responsibility and action.

Curiously enough, these same surging waves of numbers also create an impression of urgency — almost a mental state of siege. And yet this is an unusual urgency because it is not attached to any practical sense of the obligation to deal with the cause. It is as if we are addicted to the emotion of urgency for its own sake, and so rush on, from fast emotion to fast emotion, in a directionless manner.

Which brings me back to the false, Manichaean question: if today is filled with an urgent reality, is not time spent in the past self-indulgent?

But the past is not the past. It is the context. The past — memory — is one of the most powerful, practical tools available to a civilized democracy. There is a phrase that has been used over the centuries by various writers in various countries: History is an unbroken line from the past through the present into the future. It reminds us of our successes and failures, of their context; it warns us, encourages us. Without memory we are a society suffering from advanced Alzheimer's, tackling each day like a baby with its finger stuck out before the flames.

Each time I hear one of those speeches that invoke Canada, the new country, I am reminded of our self-imposed Alzheimer's. New? It is more than four centuries since the Aboriginals, francophones and anglophones began their complex intercourse in this place. We are the second- or third-oldest continuous democracy in the world — 152 years without civil war or coup d'état. Look around at our allies. Compare.

Each of us, through birth or immigration, brings something new to this experience. We add. We change. But for better and for worse, we do not erase. Only ideological dictatorships erase.

With the past we can see trajectories through into the future — both catastrophic and creative projections. The central trajectory of the modern Canadian democratic society has its foundations in the great reform alliance of Louis LaFontaine and Robert Baldwin; and indeed in that of Joseph Howe, which brought democracy to Nova Scotia a month before LaFontaine formed his responsible government on March 1848.

The words *responsible government* so underplay the importance of the event that we miss its real meaning: the responsibility is that of the government to the people's representatives; 1848 was the moment when the very legitimacy of our society was switched from the colonial elites to the citizens.

Of course it was a flawed democracy. Women without the vote. Not even all men. But in the context of that time the suffrage was large compared with what existed in other countries. The high levels of land ownership — you needed land to survive — meant the electorate that chose Howe, LaFontaine, Baldwin was dominated by poor, largely illiterate farmers. They had a sophisticated idea of their own ambitions and responsibilities.

What gives meaning to the arrival of democracy is not the event itself; not the abstract action of voting; certainly not the power-oriented idea of majorities. What made this the key to our past, present and future was the context that surrounded the event.

The reformers sought democracy because they imagined a certain kind of society. Ils avaient un projet de société. If you take today's apparently abstract "situation" of poverty — of child poverty, for example — and place it in the context of the intent of 1848, it takes on real meaning. Meaning as to what the concept of democracy is intended to include in this society.

Joseph Howe:

The only questions I ask myself are, What is right?
What is just? What is for the public good?

I would press any ministry of which I was a member
to take the initiative . . . in every noble enterprise, to
be in advance of the social, political and industrial
energies which we have undertaken to lead.

Robert Baldwin warned of "the consequences of that
reckless disregard of the first principles of [democracy
and justice] which, if left unchecked, can lead but to
widespread social disorganization with all its fearful
consequences."

And from Louis LaFontaine, in what for me is the
cornerstone document of modern Canada — his Address
to the Electors of Terrebonne in 1840 — these words,
which cannot be repeated enough:

Pour nous empêcher d'en jouir, il faudrait détruire
l'égalité sociale qui forme le caractère distinctif tant
de la population du Haut-Canada que de celle du
Bas-Canada. Car cette égalité sociale doit nécessaire-
ment amener notre liberté politique. . . . Il ne peut
exister au Canada aucune caste privilégiée en dehors
et au-dessus de la masse de ses habitants.

The only way that the authorities can prevent us from succeeding is by destroying the social equality that is the distinctive characteristic as much of the populations of Upper Canada as of Lower Canada. This social equality must necessarily bring our political liberty. . . . No privileged caste can exist in Canada beyond and above the mass of its inhabitants.

Is this romanticism? Of course LaFontaine knew there would always be richer and poorer. But he — they — were inventing the idea of a profoundly middle-class society, in which that middle class would be as inclusive as possible. And they were centring it not on the European idea of the self-interested bourgeoisie but on a rather peculiar new idea of what Baldwin called "the happy conduct of public affairs." Happy — in the eighteenth-century sense — meaning the fulfillment of the common weal.

What sounds romantic today was to many infuriating. The quasi-totality of the Canadian elites did everything they could to deny political power to the democrats — or call them the humanists or the reformers or the advocates of happiness, that is, of the public good. And for almost eight years the reformers refused the blandishments of

power. Or rather they wouldn't trade their principles
for power. By today's standards of *realpolitik* they were
stubborn and weak. They lacked ego and ambition. They
stuck to their principles.

We often say that compromise is a Canadian virtue,
that compromise has got us through the difficult situation
of our complex population, complex internal geography
and complex foreign relations. It was the reform leadership of 150 years ago that developed this idea of compromise. But their idea had nothing to do with our
contemporary use of the word to describe self-interested
negotiations through which each of the stakeholders gets
a piece of the pie. Nothing to do with shared selfishness
bought at the expense of the public weal.

Their compromise was based upon confidence in
the people and an understanding of the principles at
stake. Baldwin spoke of "that forbearance, moderation
and firmness on the part of the people which, so long
as it compromises no great principle, affords the best
assurance of the possession of fitness for the exercise of
political power."

And so, when the citizens did at last give them power,
it was based upon the solid foundations of a shared
understanding of the operating principles of the society.
Over the next three years — a mere three years — they

changed, reformed, revolutionized in every direction. They put in place the foundations of modern Canada.

This hall is surrounded by Robert Baldwin's university. It was consciously designed by him to remove higher education from the hands of the colonial elites — that is, the religious, financial and social elites. The intent was to create a broadly based, disinterested public education, and it became the model for Canada's higher learning. In other words, he put in place the idea of universities as necessarily public institutions.

It's just worth remembering today, when the very ideal of the independent public university is in question, that Baldwin's reform faced violent attacks. There were, as there still are, those who thought a less public system would permit opportunities for personal profit and influence. Among them, Bishop Strachan — whose Trinity College lies a few metres from here — argued that such a university would "place all forms of error on an equality with truth, by patronizing equally . . . an unlimited number of sects, whose doctrines are absolutely irreconcilable. . . . [S]uch a fatal departure from all that is good is without a parallel in the history of the world."

The beginning of a fully funded, universal public school system was also put in place. They understood that this was — and this remains — the key to our functioning democracy. They extended the principles of responsible government into the towns, villages and townships. This creation of municipal democracy involved a great decentralization of power and of responsibility, a second democratic revolution meant to bring legitimacy so close to the people that no authority could remove it. They reorganized the judicial system, including key legislation on trial by jury. They decentralized the trial system so that justice was available to the majority of the population for whom a trip to town was an economic burden. Both in Canada and in Nova Scotia they opened up the railway system, beginning our transportation revolution. They put through our equivalent of an anti–rotten borough bill. They removed primogeniture, a self-inflicted blow, given Baldwin's own interests as a man of property. It was a government in the best tradition of the Republic of Dubrovnik, which had lasted a thousand years. Over the door of that city state's Great Council were the words "Forget your business and attend to the public one."

There were dozens of other basic changes that even today decide the shape of our society. But let me come back to a key point: the real meaning of that word *compromise*. Not trade-offs, but moderation in the light of basic principles. When the Château Clique and their allies came out into the streets of Montreal on the night on April 25, 1849, and burnt down the Parliament of Canada, the government responded with moderation. Everywhere else in the West, governments automatically responded to such situations with rifles and cannon. The Executive Council — the cabinet — met on the twenty-seventh in the midst of the ongoing disorder and ratified a report that would explain their policy. It stated that "the proper mode of preserving order is by strengthening the Civil Authorities." And that the "Council deprecate the employment of the Military to suppress such disturbances . . ."

It was one of those perfectly existential moments. Here was a fragile half colony/half country, which already had two languages, as well as many ethnic groups and religions — without even taking into account the Aboriginal role as a founding member of the society. In nineteenth-century terms it was a powder keg. The government's response would cause this place either to slip down the European/American road towards impossible oppositions, outright violence and a centralized monolithic model, or the ministers would have to discover another way.

Somehow, LaFontaine and Baldwin reached down into their own ethics and imaginations and decided upon

an original and much criticized response. The imperial
government in London, for example, was furious that the
streets had not been cleared with volleys of rifle fire. The
great western historian W. L. Morton has put it that the
reformers decided "not to answer defiance with defiance,
but to have moderate conduct shame arrogant violence."
It was the nuanced sophistication of their response that
made possible today's complex society.

Now, many people here tonight could rise to point
out examples of violence in our history or a lack of
ethical behaviour or of non-respect for minorities. And I
would agree. Have there been failures? Yes. Great injustices ignored? Absolutely. Betrayals? Unfortunately, yes.
Hypocrisy? Waves of it. After all, what I am describing is
a real society, not a nationalistic publicity stunt. And the
point of memory is also to remember the failures. And
to judge these against the main trajectory of society.
Each time we do not respond with "moderate conduct"
to justified or unjustified provocation, we inflict a new
suppurating wound on ourselves, and it alters our
memory. Most societies are destroyed by the accumu-
lated weight of their self-inflicted wounds. It could be
argued that by the standards of Western civilization our
wounds are infrequent and small. Still, they are there.
They are real. And they never disappear.

However, the obvious point about the reformers is that they succeeded. The burning of the Parliament buildings was one of our greatest successes — or, rather, the way it was handled was a great success. And the Lord Durham school of doom and gloom about what these minorities would do to each other turned out, quite simply, to be wrong.

What's more, once you have focused on the remarkable success story of the late 1840s and early '50s, you can't help rethinking the almost religious status conferred upon a few of our Fathers of Confederation. They are habitually presented to us as the creators of a country out of dust in 1867, propelled forward only by the impatient leadership of the imperial government and by their own imaginations and ambitions. In truth, they operated with their imaginations dominated not by London or Paris or the neighbours to the south, or, indeed, by the failures of Mackenzie and Papineau, but by the successful model that LaFontaine and Baldwin and Howe had created twenty years before. The concern of the Fathers of Confederation — both those who supported Confederation and those who opposed it, including Howe — was that they would fail to live up to that model. Some did. Some didn't. What was the model? Let me summarize it in this way: After 133 years of this unusual experiment, we have killed in political strife among ourselves less than a hundred citizens — most of them on a single day at Batoche.

Even one is, of course, one too many. But compared with any other Western democracy, the number is almost miraculous. You may consider this an odd reflection, but I think the first measure of any citizen-based culture must be not its rhetoric or myths or leaders or laws but how few of its own citizens it kills.

Nineteenth-century statesmen read a good deal of Greek literature. When exactly, how exactly, did LaFontaine and Baldwin find the right way to respond that night, as Montreal exploded? I like to think that one of them had been reading Euripides — *The Bacchae* — and had noted the solid advice of Teresias:

> [P]ay heed to my words. You rely
> On force; but it is not force that governs human
>   affairs.
> Do not mistake for wisdom that opinion which
> May rise from a sick mind. . . .
> [I]n all matters, self-control
> Resides in our own natures.

At this point you might think that I've taken us quite a way away from those four to five thousand people who are close around us in this city tonight and yet are without homes. Not at all. I've been talking about the foundations of your society and mine, foundations built upon a conscious intellectual concept of, and therefore dependent upon, ethics and principle. These principles assume moderation, inclusion and citizen-based legitimacy.

I therefore feel comfortable saying that on the basis of such a foundation, it is not possible to imagine that such a state of poverty — of exclusion — as four to five thousand homeless a night in one city is normal or part of the way things have to be.

To which someone might reply that things have changed, conditions have changed, technology, global markets, interdependency. We can no longer be held responsible for our past engagements? I won't go on. You know the line. In reply I could, without trying to avoid our failures, nevertheless trace the LaFontaine-Baldwin trajectory event by event, over the past 152 years.

There is the prairie farmer reform movement of the early twentieth century that took up the inclusive ideal of the early reformers and redefined it for the twentieth century, for all of Canada, introducing everything from votes for women to transfer payments to medicare. I could even argue that le modèle québécois is in large part the result of the prairie farmers' model — and that is a compliment to both parties.

And out of that prairie movement I could trace the evolution of Clifford Sifton, the great newspaper baron, capitalist and politician who organized the settlement of the west under Laurier. You would hear him speaking out in the late 1920s about our drift away from this society's real trajectory; about "frenzied finance . . . the purpose of which is to inflate the capital of corporations serving the public, and to load onto the public the subsequent necessity of paying dividends on inflated capital." Along the way he clarified the role of the press: "It is no part of a newspaper's function to defend a corporation; a corporation is always well able to defend itself."

And out of that I could trace the career of the greatest philosopher and economist Canada has yet produced — Harold Innis, of Robert Baldwin's university — saying, in a multitude of ways, "[M]aterialism is the auxiliary doctrine of every tyranny."

And parallel to that, the remarkable Monseigneur Charbonneau, Archevêque de Montréal, standing up in his cathedral on May 1, 1949, during the Asbestos strike and preaching before a hostile premier and establishment that "nous nous attachons plus à l'homme qu'au capital. . . . [Q]ue l'on cesse d'accorder plus d'attention aux intérêts d'argent qu'à l'élément humain."

Of course, that is still fifty years ago, and the counter-argument would still be that since then things have changed. Things have changed is the standard answer to any suggestion that memory is important.

Let me deal, therefore, with this idea that something called progress or change can wipe out something called memory or the trajectory of a society. The underlying idea seems to be that for the first time in twenty-five hundred years of Western civilization things have changed so drastically that the public good must automatically give way before technology and self-interest. This argument reminds me of what Robert Baldwin called the struggle of "the might of public opinion against fashion and corruption."

Of course things have changed. They have always changed. Sometimes more, sometimes less. But nothing has happened over the past quarter century that has had an unredeemable, inevitable, searing effect on our link to our past. On our ability to enforce our ethical standards. Or on the power of citizens to engage in responsible individualism. It is an insult to our intelligence and to the redeeming value of positive change to suggest that we are its passive victim, that it *must* dehumanize us and separate us from the reality of our ethics.

Let me give you three examples of the deforming nature that change can have when it is treated as a great avenging god. The phenomenon that I call corporatism has affected the ability of every sector of society to act. Indeed, we have all become used to acting out our specialist dramas within our specialist relationships. In that way, whether in Europe or Australia or North America, society has truly been divided into interest groups — some of them against the public good, some indifferent, some in favour, but all acting outside of the inclusive mechanisms of democracy.

Think of areas such as social work or environmentalism. These subjects fill the airwaves, fill the newspapers. We have the impression that we have learnt a great deal about the problems these movements deal with — from the homeless to pollution. In Sydney, in Paris, here, in Berlin, we sense a certain agreement for action within the society. And yet that action, when it does come, rarely matches the strength of the movement or the public support for it. But, and this is my point, if we turn to our elected assemblies — at all levels and indeed in almost all countries — we discover that there are very few elected social workers or environmentalists.

In the late nineteenth century, parliaments, such as the French Assembly, the Canadian House of Commons, the American House of Representatives, were filled with lawyers, because we were busy putting in place the necessary legal infrastructures. Today, in most assemblies, lawyers represent only some 15 percent of the elected representatives; managers of various sorts have increased to 15 percent; business people another 15 percent. But, for example, in Ottawa, only two MPs identify themselves as environmentalists. And I'm sure that they won't mind my pointing out that they belong to the first wave of environmentalists. The younger generations are not in the democratic process. They are caught up in their parallel work in NGOs [non-governmental organizations], as are the social workers.

Now, NGO work is fascinating. It is good work. But the structures being used are corporatist. And we live, throughout the West, in democracies — that is, in places in which changes are made through the democratic process. In a curious way, the very success of those NGOs most devoted to the public good actually undermines the democratic process — the real guarantor of the public good — because they don't feed into it.

I'm not suggesting that elected houses be reduced to collections of interest groups. I'm saying that reform tends to come when the reformers integrate themselves into the democratic process. If they stay outside, they reduce themselves to lobbyists — and a lobbyist is a lobbyist is a lobbyist, whether the cause is good or bad. The problem is that the courtier-like features required to be an effective lobbyist are usually better suited to causes that undermine the public good than to those that support it.

So long as a good cause is outside the political process, it will be subject to the argument that there isn't the money, or there are other priorities or, inevitably, that things have changed. Let me put this argument a different way. So long as an NGO — which could also be defined as a corporation of social reformers — remains outside the democratic system, it has no real political levers. Its activists are not there, in the people's chamber, to clarify the cause. And there is no practical link between the problem they are devoted to and the real action required to deal with it. PR victories — which NGOs so often win — cannot be converted automatically into law. Nor should they be. Again, we live in democracies. But the result is that there are no direct practical links between the public debate and government action. The public therefore becomes discouraged about the effectiveness of politics, because politics appear to be unresponsive to the public debate. And because of their disconnection from the formal political process, the corporations of social reformers themselves begin to look naive. All of this results in what playwright René-Daniel Dubois calls "la perte d'une culture partagée" — a fractured culture or a fractured society.

Before you know it, poverty has been intellectually reconfigured into a condition of society — an inevitability — while at a human level it is treated as a personal failure. Suddenly society seems unable to respond with nuanced sophistication to what actually is natural and inevitable about human beings — that is, differences in personality, in ambition, in mental aptitude, in opportunities.

In other words, so long as a good cause remains on the outside, it may actually give comfort to those who oppose it. A cause really only makes ethical, utilitarian and social sense when it and its proponents are integrated into the democratic process. I'm not suggesting the NGOs have no valid role. Involvement in democratic politics does not mean that any individual must abandon parallel reform movements. We are all capable of doing two things at once, of being two people.

The current withdrawal of most social reformers from our democratic process is certainly a change in our society, but I don't think it was inevitable or is eternal. It is merely a side effect of corporatism. Once we realize that, and realize that both democracy and the causes of reform are suffering, well, a realignment will begin.

A second example: fashion throughout the West has it that we must move away from overarching, all-inclusive public programs in favour of targeted programs. But the targeting of need — which is what it comes down to — takes us back to the old top-down, judgmental and eventually moralizing approach towards those citizens who have problems. In fact, this is false efficiency because it removes the simplicity of inclusion and replaces it with an outdated, highly charged, labour-intensive managerial approach.

I'm not suggesting that our current systems don't have problems. But these have nothing to do with "universality" or ethical inclusiveness. They have to do with the weakness of rational linear management.

The point of targeted programs is that they not only bring back judgmental administration, they bring back plain old charity. This is now presented as citizens taking on more responsibility for others. But if they can afford that responsibility, they can afford the taxes that would ensure we do not slip into a society of noblesse oblige in which those *with* get to choose who and how to help those *without.*

As Strindberg put it in his blunt and accurate way, "All charity is humiliating." Perhaps it isn't surprising that charity was one of the weapons used by the opponents of Canadian democracy in the 1840s. Sir Charles Metcalfe, the autocratic governor general, was famous for his largesse as he attempted to buy support. He was lauded by the anti-democratic elites as "a fortune spender in public charity."

Ethics is quite different. It doesn't require the gratitude of the recipient, i.e., the humiliation of the recipient. The ego of the donor is not stroked. There is no warm, self-indulgent feeling of having done good. Ethics is a much cooler business than charity. That is why the concept of arm's length goes with that of the public good. Ethics is about citizens being treated equally. And in that sense, it is all important that we concentrate on the difference between the role of the citizen and that of the state. The citizen owns the state and receives from it neither charity nor the generosity of noblesse oblige. What the citizen receives is meant to be, as Baldwin put it, appropriate to "the happy conduct of public affairs."

I'm not suggesting for a moment that there is no room for charity. Or that the line between charity and obligation is ever clear. But charity cannot replace, in an inclusive democracy, the organization of the public good. And if it does, well, then it excludes citizens from their role as citizens because they are dependent on another.

Citizenship is about obligation, not about choosing to be generous.

But then *things have changed.* We are told that because of globalization we can no longer count on the obligation of the citizen. For example, apparently we can no longer count on nation states being able to raise taxes in a competitive world economy. And so increasingly we must hope that generous individuals will give as best they can. In fact, our ability to apply the idea of obligation to citizenship is fatally weakened because, we are told, the nation state as we have known it is finished. Has been severely weakened. Is probably on its way out.

It is very curious. I have noticed that the people who talk most triumphantly of the victory of democracy over various ideologies are the same people who talk about the nation state being dead, powerless, or words to that effect. They often manage their triumphalism and their dirge in the same paragraph.

But the thing is this. Democracy was and is entirely constructed inside the structure of the Western nation state. Democracy is an emanation of the nation state. And now that most of the unpleasant nationalist, racial, imperial characteristics of our nations have been eliminated, democracy, citizenship, obligation and the public good remain as their greatest glory.

The other curious thing is that those who announce the death of the nation state usually do so with a little self-satisfied smile.

Well, if the nation state is dead, so is democracy. Then it is not the state that has passed away, but the power of the citizen. And passed away in favour of what? Of the transnational? Nobody could take such an argument seriously unless their income depended in some way on believing that the nation state was finished.

I don't think that this chronicle of a death foretold is accurate. And not because I believe in the force or virtues of nationalism. Rather, I believe in the aggressive intelligence of the citizenry, as against the ultimately self-destructive nature of corporatism and the passive, inefficient, top-heavy directionlessness of the transnational. Individuals have not struggled centuries to establish an idea of responsibility and a sense of the concrete, inclusive public good in order to give it all away simply because some transient technology and heavy-handed interest groups have been declared by mysterious, unknown forces to be in charge.

In any case, what is presented today as a great monolithic absolute truth called Globalization is merely one particular, indeed narrow, version of internationalism. There are dozens of other possible versions. There is nothing brilliant or inevitable about this particular model. If anything, it resembles an unsophisticated version of late-nineteenth-century dogma.

Frankly, it doesn't even meet its own standards. It is declared to be a victory for the marketplace, yet it is rushing towards monopolies and oligopolies in sector after sector. Anyone who is in favour of capitalism and competition must be against these old monopolistic forms. We know that, among other things, private-sector monopolies make up for their ineffectiveness by limiting progress in order to create an illusion of stability.

In any case, we can already see the nation states reacting. On the negative side, there is the return of false populism. Austria is just the latest example, and this phenomenon is in part a protest against the citizen's sense of powerlessness.

On the positive side, a great deal more is happening. There are early but widespread moves underway to regulate the international money markets. Australia has balked at engaging in a number of the recent economic fashions. New Zealand, the fairy tale of the economic determinists, is reversing directions. One senses the leadership of the G7 growing nervous over the power of the unregulated transnationals. Even the OECD is calling for controls. I'm not suggesting that we are headed back to 1960. Or that we should be. I am saying that the force at the core of our trajectory — and that of many other countries — is the citizenry. And they have been presented with an unrealistic picture in which economics has been internationalized through dozens of complex binding treaties, while democracy, social policy, most of justice, work conditions and taxation powers have been left, hobbled, at the national level.

The citizens will either require changes to the international economic arrangements that will permit, for example, sufficient levels of national taxation and regulation. Or they will require international agreements in all of those other areas. Or some combination of the two.

Too late, some will say. No turning back now. Things have changed. Globalization is inevitable.

Well, for better and for worse, nothing is inevitable. Only ideologues believe in determinism. And economic fashions usually last no more than twenty-five years. Besides, the moment something is declared to be inevitable, you know you are approaching a major swing around, often in the opposite direction.

And now, let me offer a third and final portrait of fashion pretending to be revolutionary change. It goes like this. The world is one small place, therefore everything in it must be big. Big companies and big government departments. Everything must be merged to meet the challenge of global smallness. The logic is hazy. The theory, however, is that these continual mergers and the rapid emergence of monopolies and oligopolies is a logical outcome of the international marketplace. This is nonsense from a business point of view. The best way to progress, function, make profits in such a large single market is to be small or medium-sized — that is, to be fast and flexible. The worst is to be a slow, directionless technocratic haven. Even as these mergers go crashing on — and failing at a rate of about 80 percent — you can sense a more intelligent undercurrent in the marketplace going in the opposite direction.

The truth is that gigantism — which is what we are now experiencing — is a managerial ideal. It has nothing to do with the market. It has to do with the standard, late-nineteenth-century, technocratic technique in which power equals control and more power equals a need for control over a larger structure. Gigantism is pure form over content, to say nothing of personal self-indulgence for a few individuals. It is also a fashion that will probably last less than a decade.

In any case, it is expansion in the absence of ideas. A few months ago in Australia I came across a vibrant advertisement on the hoarding around a large expansion building site for a department store chain.

DAVID JONES
Bringing you an exciting
Shopping experience
for the
New Millennium

If you haven't got anything else to do for the next thousand years, why not?

The point is that very large corporations do not work as effective players in a competitive marketplace. They are slow, inefficient and seek monopoly or oligopoly status. Very large government departments do a bit better, as their purpose is the administration of vast non-competitive services. But they have difficulty giving direction. And public policy works only when it is driven by ideas. When it is driven by form and management, it collapses.

I'd like to close tonight with the possibility of a real change — one that relates to the trajectory of our society. It is as relevant to our past as to our future — both to the citizen's role, whether homeless or comfortable, and to making sense of globalization.

The brief description I gave a little while ago of LaFontaine and Baldwin's three-year government was that of a massive consolidation of the ideas that had been in the air for years. I spoke after that of the key role lawyers played in our nineteenth-century parliaments. They were organizing a society in desperate need of legal shape. But already, in his resignation speech in September 1851, Louis LaFontaine was talking about the need for law reform.

> Le danger aujourd'hui, c'est la facilité avec laquelle on fait des lois. Si l'on continue, notre code sera bientôt un labyrinthe dans lequel personne ne pourra se retrouver.

Joseph Howe was a little funnier on the same subject.

> Every law could be reduced to half its size and made twice as effective. A reward should be offered for the best and smallest act on any subject.

I'll give you a contemporary example of this. As a writer, I really ought to understand the libel laws. I don't. Neither do most lawyers. But how can you have effective freedom of speech if nobody can understand its legal limits?

What I am talking about is much more than law reform. For half a century we have been busy putting in place, on an ad hoc basis, structures and programs that have successfully produced a reasonably just society, at least in comparison with what came before. This ad hoc method is normal in a democracy. Each small advance is the result of debate and then of legislation.

Our accomplishments, however, now resemble a large mound filled with legal and administrative details. For most people, whether citizens on the outside or working on the inside, it is an impenetrable mass. There is never a view of the whole, or even of an entire single logic within the whole.

The more complex this has become, the more it has encouraged the worst in our managerial societies. By that I mean a narrow corporatist approach — a world of consultants and of specialist dialects, of stakeholders and of confused, frustrated citizens. And more and more ad hoc changes.

Not surprisingly, as the mound builds up, the managerial solutions tend to deal increasingly with narrow issues, one at a time, and in the short term. That is one of the explanations for why we have regressed into need-based programs.

What I am describing is a curiosity of democratic societies. We start out with a long view and a desire to create inclusive programs. Democracy, rightfully, requires that we create them in an ad hoc manner. Over the short term this is fine. But if we leave them in an ad hoc form, they gradually become the opposite of what we originally intended.

Perhaps the most important job to be done over the past twenty years was to take this enormous ad hoc mound of law and regulation and administrative detail and to consolidate it — to clarify, boil down, rediscover the shape of it. This was not done. The result would have been, could still be, to reunite the citizens with their state.

At first a project like this doesn't sound too exciting. But the obscurity of the mound is one of the key elements preventing citizens from participating as citizens. And consolidation is always the essential second step to be taken after an initial chaotic rush to reform. Most of the programs we have put in place in the democratic manner still work surprisingly well, especially considering their structure. But those who believe in the original reforms have made the mistake over the past few years of defending the ad hoc jumble of their form rather than the underlying principles. As a result, most reforms undertaken over the past twenty years in the name of efficiency have actually resulted in less delivery of programs and more cost. Why? Because they are an attempt to micromanage large, complex subjects.

These contemporary false reformers should have been in the forefront of the battle for consolidation, flying the flag of ideas, intent and ethics. Instead they have defended structure and so have found themselves marginalized by those who do not believe and who use the now unnecessary complexity of the mound as an excuse to undo the actual accomplishments of the reforms.

There was a desperate need twenty years ago — a need that is now even more desperate — to take that leap into consolidation. If such a consolidation were to be successful, it would prepare the way for a whole new wave of creative reforms. And I believe that those reforms would take the shape of clear, overarching and determinedly inclusive policies. Fewer, but all-inclusive, programs would be far cheaper and far more effective.

I'm not suggesting for a moment that four to five thousand homeless people in Toronto will have to wait for those changes in order to see their situation improve. But I am certain that we would see this whole problem quite differently if we saw it in the light of clear, simple, inclusive policies. One of the hardest things to do in public policy is to marry ethics with effective programs. The cool arm's-length approach of ethics combined with simple, clear, all-inclusive policies can make that happen. And that would be an honest reflection of the trajectory that Louis LaFontaine and Robert Baldwin sent our way.

∼ Conversation One

RUDYARD GRIFFITHS: Let's start by discussing the future of the concepts of democracy and citizenship. In your respective lectures, it seems that these notions of citizenship and civic agency are being challenged. They're being challenged by globalism, by consumerism, by nationalism. And I'm wondering if the three of you can comment on where you see citizenship going. Is the model envisaged by LaFontaine and Baldwin of the engaged kind of egalitarian citizen still viable in Canada? Is it a model we need to rethink or change? And what are the obstacles to an open, active and thoughtful practice of citizenship in Canada today? Who would like to start?

ALAIN DUBUC: I will. I think that citizenship is a relative concept, not an absolute one. Citizenship is about common values, but it's also about identity, and this is not something that was thought about in the past. Obviously, we see it burgeoning with the French, and we also now see it with immigrants who do not so readily accept shedding their culture when they arrive in Canada. So we have to deal with the fact that new Canadians won't be Canadian in the same way; they won't see Canada in the same way. That's one problem.

The second problem is that some people will have multiple identities and so will be Canadian in their own way. This is true for the French and it will also be true for new Canadians. Probably the notion of identity will evolve for Canadians, the classical English-speaking Canadians themselves, in relation to the different parts of the country they inhabit and in relation to the world. Are they North American? Are they world citizens? And in the way we see all countries evolve, I think that we have to deal with a kind of puzzle where nobody will be able to define themselves as a Canadian.

RUDYARD GRIFFITHS: So no one will have an exclusive licence on citizenship.

JOHN RALSTON SAUL: When I go out and talk to people, I sense an enormous frustration in citizens, and it has many sounds: an Aboriginal is frustrated, a francophone is frustrated, a new Canadian is frustrated. Nobody is talking to them about how they're going to be citizens and how they're going to fit in. People feel that there isn't really a role for them to play except to vote, or very, very minimal participation. In terms of decisions that are going to be made — the major decisions — you can't say much. The small decisions you might have an impact on. So there's a central question. Are we going to find a positive way to be citizens, or are we going to be reactive and angry? What you're starting to see in Europe is an increasing rise of anger among the citizens who feel left out. You can see that happening politically throughout Europe in a very serious way.

On the other hand, Canada, since it arose from a relatively intellectual idea of how to put together a country, actually isn't a bad foundation from which to think about being a citizen in the future. We accept that you can have group rights, you can have individual rights, et cetera. The hard part is that we have to be linked together by a concept of what holds us together, as opposed to race or language or region. We can also have all those things, or any variety of them. I actually think Canadians are quite comfortable with this idea of citizenship as a hand of cards.

I'll put it slightly differently. It's as if everybody knows they've got a hand of cards — you're a Dene, you're from the Northwest Territories, you're a Canadian — and they can just go down this list and play any card at any time, or any number of cards at any time. Canadians are comfortable with that, but I'm not sure that the formal structures are comfortable with it.

GEORGES ERASMUS: I think that because Canada as a country is still very young, there's a lot of growth that's still going to happen. The influence from Aboriginal people in the country is still just starting to be felt. The characteristics of the major institutions are mainly non-Aboriginal: they're hierarchical, they create power imbalances. I suspect that as time goes on, you're going to find that with Nunavut and other parts of the Northwest Territories, the Yukon, perhaps the Prairie provinces and so forth, you're going to get some structures that are less hierarchical and you're going to create situations where the values are more influenced by Aboriginal people.

I strongly agree that there will continue to be people that identify more strongly with regions — like Newfoundland or Quebec or the Dene area of the Northwest Territories — so they will consider themselves that before they call themselves Canadians.

This experiment that we're all involved in is still very young, but we're bringing in new people all the time, and a lot of these people continue to be citizens of the places they came from. We've even seen in the past couple of decades people leaving here to go and join struggles back in their homelands. . . .

RUDYARD GRIFFITHS: Yugoslavia is a good example.

GEORGES ERASMUS: Yes, they might run for office over there, that kind of thing. So you're going to continue to have that kind of dual citizenship, with Canadians remaining citizens elsewhere. But even within Canada, I've always thought that if we were prepared to look at the Quebec question with a bit more openness, we would easily see the people in Quebec being citizens of Quebec first and then citizens of Canada, and it would play really nicely to what Aboriginal people have been trying to get the country to consider for quite some time. The Aboriginal people want to continue to maintain their nationhood. So their citizens would be citizens of their own nation as well as citizens of Canada.

An idea we proposed in the *Report of the Royal Commission on Aboriginal Peoples* [1996] was kind of interesting. We suggested that one of the ways this might be addressed would be carrying passports that first recognize that you're a citizen of the particular nation you're from — a Dene or a Cree or a Nisga'a — and then the Canadian passport, which you could also use.

This would make it possible for many Aboriginal people to start looking at Canada in a different way. We still have many Aboriginal people who will tell you they're not Canadian. The same is true in Quebec, as you know very well. But unless we have the opportunity sometime down the road for this to be addressed, we will continue to have this discussion.

There is definitely something we're all doing together as Canadians. The evolution of our character is not mature, not by any means, and that's partly the reason why we feel so imbalanced all the time. We seem to be knocked over fairly quickly with any kind of strong leanings. You know, we're on the defensive about Quebec, we're defensive about Aboriginal people.

We're bringing in new people, but how do we identify ourselves? We're not American. But we don't need to identify ourselves in the negative, as if we don't know who we are and say what we're not. And I suspect that the growth we're going to go through is going to be quite profound. In the next fifty years, we will start to see the end of some of the issues involving Aboriginal people, and maybe even those in Quebec. When these kinds of issues are actually challenged and dealt with, we can get to another stage.

RUDYARD GRIFFITHS: Let's talk about what that other stage might be. Your Excellency, in your speech . . .

JOHN RALSTON SAUL: But just before, I do think that if you're looking at mechanisms, you have to be very conscious that you only have a certain number of mechanisms in any society. And about the only fully functioning mechanism we have that allows new Canadians to join in in some way, and different kinds of Canadians to join in with each other in some way, is the public education system, because most of the others have been severely weakened. Now that's not actually true, because you can stand back and say that there are nation structures among Aboriginals that might be smaller, so they could actually act the way a city state acted in the past, and you'll find all sorts of exceptions such as that. Take Lac St-Jean, Quebec, for example. It's small enough in population that people can feel they're part of an identifiable community. But the vast majority of the population have difficulty finding structures that allow them to have a discussion with themselves. The only time when you can really give citizens an idea of how they fit together is during those first twelve years of school, and then maybe the next four years if they go to university. I think that if a country like Canada loses or endangers that basic principle of universal public education in any way, it will be virtually impossible to make any of what we're discussing work. It would just fly apart, because there would be nothing that could feed the different parts in together.

RUDYARD GRIFFITHS: Let's talk about that, and, Alain, maybe you can comment. How do we hold it together? We understand the importance of these multiple identities, as you've said, the need to give them articulation and expression, but we need some kind of support, or a series of supports, to bring that common project of expressing multiple identities together. Coming from Quebec, where do you see, outside of Quebec, those supports that will hold Quebec in the country but will allow for, in a sense, a multiple identity to emerge and to be validated?

ALAIN DUBUC: It depends. When we talk about situations, we also talk about identity, and identity is defined by the state and by some institutions. It's also defined by values, and what I'm slowly learning about Canada and Quebec is that people hold some strong values, stronger than those put forward by governments and institutions. We see, in the negative way, how Canadians do not want to be, and at least that's a sign that there's a will to do something. I don't think that the way it's expressed is always useful, but I'd like to make a simple acknowledgement that different Canadians can be Canadian in different ways. And if the Canadian model were more eclectic, there would be fewer problems.

JOHN RALSTON SAUL: I don't know, Georges, what you hear around the country, but one of the most common lines you hear in Nunavut is people basically saying, "We're Canadians now," and what they mean by that is that they are Canadians by choice after the agreement on Nunavut. And it's an extremely positive statement, because they actually have a definition of themselves as

Canadians that they're happy with. I don't know if you hear that said, positively or negatively.

GEORGES ERASMUS: Well, the places where you would hear it negatively would be where, for instance, issues have not been resolved — treaties have not been settled, old treaties need to be revisited, land claims have not happened — where the issues still need to be clarified. It's going to be a challenge for that to be seriously addressed, but it can be addressed.

JOHN RALSTON SAUL: I think if you look at that, and if you look at what Alain is saying, what's interesting is that something like public education is not an institution that tells you what to do. It's not supposed to, at any rate. It's supposed to be an institution in which you can express yourself. It's difficult, but people can meet and things can happen. It's not an institution that is supposed to make everybody into the same thing — at least in Canada, it's not supposed to.

But there is no question that we have a lot of trouble accommodating the differences people are happy with, along with the values that they actually share. That's the thing that strikes me, going across the country. People are very happy in all the things that make them different — it's a positive to them. And they are also very happy that they share these other things that tend to be more abstract, abstract in the sense that they're a value, an idea, an approach that fits into whatever the differences are. The problem is to find a way of expressing that.

ALAIN DUBUC: It's the problem that Baldwin and LaFontaine were aware of. Not only that, but they were able to say so at the same time in our history — they were able to capture common values, or at least the common goals. And if there's a problem — if people have problems expressing their situation — then if politics redefines itself in some way . . .

RUDYARD GRIFFITHS: Your Excellency, in your speech you said you see a problem with the NGO community, in that it takes on some of the impetus for the articulation of values, and discussions of values, but then it acts entirely outside of Parliament and the democratic process.

JOHN RALSTON SAUL: You know, when I said that, that was actually the first time I'd ever said it and I expected to be stoned. In that hall I think there were probably 50 percent of the people who belonged to one NGO or another, and they seemed to be nodding. I think that people in the NGO community know that, on the one hand, it was and still is a very valid position to be outside of the mainstream of politics on whatever issue interests you, but that at some point the discussion has to bleed into, integrate into the mainstream political parties, start parties, go into parties, go into the mainstream political debate, because otherwise you are siphoning off energy from the mainstream political debate. How does a citizen support a reform, which after all needs to become a law, or an administration or a policy? How do they do that if there's nobody going into mainstream politics to represent it, if everybody's outside?

What you end up doing is treating politics as if it were at another level; in other words, we all stand outside and lobby, and then we sort of beg. We say, "Well, we're the majority, we're ethically right, we beg you to do something." But we haven't actually expressed our majority fully through the electoral process. It's problematic in terms of citizenship.

I'm not suggesting people leave the NGOs. Again, one can be two or three or four things at once. But there is no question that if one looks at the cities, and the people who make up the middle class, which still represents a majority in the country, a lot of people have lost the habit of soiling themselves by getting involved in the political process. Only one of the three of us here has really run for office seriously — Georges. It's a tough process.

RUDYARD GRIFFITHS: And, Georges, what's your feeling in terms of the Aboriginal community, the great pressure obviously in that community to act outside of existing parliamentary and regulatory structures because of the sense of frustration and slow pace of reform? Do you think there is still a future for Aboriginals articulating your sense of the public good within the existing framework, political and democratic?

GEORGES ERASMUS: Well, the whole issue of Aboriginal participation in the electoral process in Canada is all caught up in the understood relationship: it either exists or doesn't exist. Again, it comes back to the roots of whether Aboriginal people consider themselves Canadians, and certain ones do not. In central Canada a majority simply say no. The Iroquois Confederacy in large parts of Ontario never entered into that kind of a relationship. So until you resolve those things, the problem is that decade after decade goes by without these issues being addressed. It even extends to the Indian Act elections, where that whole concept of the Band Council was forced on Aboriginal people. Some people took to it, but many didn't, and so you still see, among the Iroquois communities in particular, only small portions of the population who bother to be involved in the elections, because as far as they are concerned it's still an imposed government and it shouldn't be the model. Until we resolve those things, I don't think you're going to have full participation.

But out west and up north, a lot of Aboriginal people will participate, and over time, with numbers changing, more and more of the ridings there are being influenced, and our people are being elected.

We have the example of the Nunavut experience where we now have a territory where the Aboriginal people wanted their own homeland, so they are participating fully there in huge, huge turnouts. It shows that if you actually do address what the Aboriginal people want, they definitely will get involved.

JOHN RALSTON SAUL: And if you add to that Nunavik, northern Quebec, and now the Cree-Quebec agreement and the Nisga'a agreement, you see that there are big pockets of what could turn into a buy-in in the full sense.

But you know, I often think that what's missing in our discussion — because we're so often talking about ourselves in terms of what we aren't — is that we don't talk enough about the kinds of contributions that areas or groups have made to the national whole. Alain, in our discussions, you talked about the unconsciousness of anglophone Canadians, not knowing they're nationalistic and thinking other people are too nationalistic and not being able to see themselves. Georges, you talked about imagining an instance of actually coming to terms with the contribution that Aboriginals made over four hundred and some years to the way the country works, because we're in denial about the shape of our democracy and where that comes from.

We really have to stop saying that we're a British parliamentary democracy with a British justice system or a French justice system. We have to stop talking in those sorts of nonsense terms and start actually looking at the way our democratic system runs, for better and worse. When you start doing that, you start seeing that there has been enormous input over hundreds of years by Aboriginals. But there has also been input by every group over a period of time. So that when I turn around and I say, "Look at modern Canadian foreign policy, at the whole idea of the honest broker, like it or not," and you say, "Well, where does that come from?" it can be acknowledged that it comes out of a very old tradition, which is probably

Aboriginal, out of the seventeenth- and eighteenth-century experience of Europeans negotiating with Aboriginals. But its modern Canadian form comes largely in the nineteenth century from francophones not wanting to go down a straight empire route. So people like [Henri] Bourassa and Laurier were part of it. And then people like Defoe, and that whole movement in the Prairies for a change in attitude at the international level. You suddenly realize that it's actually an organic part of the country. It's not something we inherited.

I'll offer one example. Consider community freezers in Nunavut. In Nunavut, you move from camps where people come in with a caribou or fish and there are five families, so there is a tradition of dividing it up. That doesn't work when you're living in a town of four to twelve hundred, so all through Nunavut (and to some extent in Nunavut it's actually a policy), each municipality has a community freezer, and if you've got leftover meat or fish that you don't need, you put it in there. Then when the caribou are coming through, you go and hunt them as a community, and you put them in the community freezer. And when people need something, they go and get it. There's no administration, there's no signing of paper, there's no humiliation. No thanks are given for the contribution and no apology is required for taking.

That's a really interesting model when you compare it with food banks in the south, which are locked up in bureaucratic justification and apologies and thanks and managed rather heavy-handedly. How would the community freezer model compare with what we're doing in Montreal or Vancouver or Toronto? We have to do more of that kind of looking around the country for models and considering whether they can be carried somewhere else.

GEORGES ERASMUS: A very similar kind of model works among the Dene community. It might be a bit more administered because the local leadership would probably be wanting the meat to be distributed at certain times of the year, because once it starts to age, the taste changes and all the rest of it. So they actually cut it all up and go around and distribute it door to door. . . . It's virtually the same, but it has the Dene twist.

JOHN RALSTON SAUL: But it replaces the model in which we say, "You're poor, you need something and we're going to give you something." It removes the charity aspect. It simply says there is extra food available for whatever reason, which is very different from the classic charity model that we have in our cities in the south here.

ALAIN DUBUC: But are you saying that this is the Canadian value? or instead does it show that you have very different values blending into a common identity, since people living in the south won't do that? It might help to know that there are some other models that work very differently.

JOHN RALSTON SAUL: I think it can be interpreted in two ways. Twenty-odd years ago, when people started setting up food banks, they thought they were doing it for a couple of months. They didn't realize it would slide into the normalization of the concept of class in our society. I think most Canadians are pretty uncomfortable with the idea of homeless shelters and food banks. I hear nobody saying it's a solution. So, in a sense, the value is shared. But because in the urban situations we're stuck in a model that is virtually a nineteenth-century class-based model, we can look at Nunavuk and say, gosh, there's an interesting model. That's pretty much what happened in the early twentieth century. The farmers on the Prairies said, look, there's another way of dealing with women's votes, transfer payments, guaranteed incomes, pricing for grain. It seemed very foreign at first to other parts of the country, but within a five-year period, they were convinced, and they changed the national agenda. It's that kind of debate about the national agenda that is fed by the most original ideas coming from different parts of the country.

Alain Dubuc

~ 2nd Annual
LaFontaine-Baldwin Lecture

École des Hautes Étude Comerciales de Montréal
Montreal, Quebec
Friday, March 9, 2001

Traduction du texte prononcé aux HEC

One year ago, I wrote a series of editorials in *La Presse*
on the political blind alley that Quebec finds itself in,

deadlocked between two political projects: the sovereigntist movement, lacking enough supporters to set in
motion a process that would lead to separation; and
the reform of federalism, with insufficient numbers of
Canadians willing to sponsor the dreamed-of constitutional changes.

My theory was that in order to escape the stalemate,
the province would have to change paradigms, to define
collective goals that fit more closely with the needs of
contemporary Quebec. But the primary obstacle to this
redeployment of priorities is the weight of a nationalism
that has not evolved in tune with society and that, with
its dogmas, its myths, its sacred cows, its empty symbols,
has become a barrier to Quebec's development.

I mention those articles because they have something
to do with my being here this evening, and because they
no doubt gave John Saul and the Dominion Institute the
idea of entrusting me with the considerable responsibility of delivering the second LaFontaine-Baldwin lecture.

As I prepared this address, my first inclination was
to elaborate on certain elements from my series of
editorials. But, after careful consideration, I changed
my mind.

First, because it would have been too easy: I'm sure
that a critique of Quebec nationalism would be a hit

with an English-Canadian audience. But this type of success wouldn't get us very far. And it would in no way mirror the spirit of my editorials, which were not meant to seduce my readers, but to force a debate on a very sensitive and very controversial subject in Quebec.

And also because it becomes tiresome, in cross-Canada forums, to be the Quebecer who presents a Quebec point of view. It's a reflection, I feel, of the sort of isolation in which Quebecers of every stripe have shut themselves up, with the result that they have taken so little interest and involved themselves so negligibly in Canadian debates that they have ceased to be relevant.

For those reasons I've chosen to speak to you not of Quebec, but of Canada. And to use my series not as a way of tackling the Quebec question, but as an analytical grid that could be used to ponder Canadian reality.

This exercise leads me to believe that the nationalisms of Canada and Quebec are close cousins, or even Siamese twins, and, despite important differences, the similarities are dramatic. Canada suffers in many respects from the same ailments as Quebec. In fact, Canadian nationalism is also in the process of congealing under the weight of myths and dogmas that are becoming obstacles to the country's evolution.

The Ills of Quebec Nationalism

I know that Quebec nationalism worries and annoys English Canada: through its militant aspects, its flags, because of the conflicts that have brought us into opposition — but also because people often tend to confuse the nationalist sentiment shared by most French-speaking Quebecers with the sovereigntist current and with the passionate outpourings and ethnocentrism of the more inflamed militants. But there are more sober ways of defining it. And one is the sense, shared by a solid majority of Quebecers, of having a distinct identity, of constituting a nation, and of wishing that this nation be recognized and have the means to fulfill itself. On these points there is great consensus in Quebec.

This sense will not disappear, and must not disappear, because it rests on a verifiable sociological reality: the existence of a people, with its dominant language, its culture, its history and institutions and its difficult relationships with the majority that demand special considerations.

The sense of constituting a nation and the will to build on it can be an extremely rich source of energy, a factor of social cohesiveness that leads to progress. But again, it is necessary that this national sense be in touch with the evolution of society. If it is static, it can be a terrible check on social progress, and if it is exalted, it can easily become a tool of exclusion rather than a window on the world. Which leads me to emphasize the necessity of distinguishing between a nationalism that is productive and modern and a nationalism that is backward-looking.

While writing my editorials, I'd thought to use the concept of good and bad nationalism and to draw a parallel, which I hoped would be humorous, with cholesterol. But friends pointed out that the world of lipids, infinitely more complex than you can imagine, does not divide cholesterols simply into the good and the bad (the example of omega-3 fatty acids will do). And when you consider the subject for any length of time, nationalism becomes a lot more complex as well.

I do not believe that present-day Quebec nationalism is reactionary. But we don't have to scratch very deep to bring those angry reflexes to life, above all in times of crisis and tension. For that force to travel in the right direction, it must be monitored, be made the subject of debate, and it must also be managed.

What struck me in the case of Quebec was that the excesses of our nationalism seemed to be explainable by the weight of history. It is normal that Quebec's national sense find its roots in the past, since the Quebec difference and the Canadian duality are the product of three centuries of history. But what is less normal is the interpretation of the history that has nourished the Quebec myth.

Our nationalism, for a long time a survival tool, was largely inspired by the numerous defeats that marked the tribulations of the French in America over the centuries, from the Plains of Abraham to Meech Lake. Its heroes are often losers: Montcalm, Dollard des Ormeaux, de Lorimier, Riel, the Patriotes, or even René Lévesque, who founded the Parti Québécois but lost his referendum.

A people must not forget where they come from. But it's not because we should be inspired by our history that we must necessarily revel in the past. This nationalism fed by history in effect created an image of ourselves that does not correspond to reality. It has perpetuated the pain of oppression long after the oppression itself disappeared. It has shaped a culture of losers, something that Quebecers have not been for quite some time. The relative oppression that French speakers have been subject to, the economic injustices they've been the victims of, a certain exclusion from the circles of power, the sense of inferiority — these have disappeared; but the memory remains, vivid enough to affect behaviours.

Wrote Paul Valéry: "History is the most dangerous product that the chemistry of the intellect ever evolved. Its properties are well known. It makes us dream, it intoxicates people, creates false memories for them, exaggerates their reactions, keeps their old wounds open, torments their rest, leads them to delusions of grandeur or of persecution, and makes nations bitter, arrogant, insufferable and vain." I have to confess that I've taken this passage to heart.

This is what we have to get rid of when breaking the chains of the past. Because the weight of history and the defeatist culture to which it gave rise continue to affect our behaviour, continue to determine our socio-political agenda, continue to colour our strategies.

For instance, remember the "humiliation" period of Lucien Bouchard, happily over. Or the contemptible "l'argent et des votes ethniques" (money and ethnic votes) that Jacques Parizeau, a man of sophistication notwithstanding, delivered himself of in a moment of despair, which had less to do with xenophobia than with the paranoia of minorities. Or again the language issue, potentially the most emotional and explosive component of the national debate, where that same attitude of the eternal loser seems to be at work.

It is also the case with Quebec's great battles. For a half century, succeeding governments in Quebec City have fought to protect provincial jurisdictions and expand their area of authority. Along with recognition of its distinct character, this has constituted one of the two major axes in Quebec's struggle to redefine its place within the federal regime.

But the way in which Quebec conducts this legitimate struggle also reflects the weight of the years.

Because of the battle that's been raging for two generations, the so-called traditional demands of Quebec are moving further and further away from the true needs of Quebecers. The matter of the sharing of powers is indeed an important one, but it still does not justify the extent of emotion reserved for it, or, more precisely, it does so no longer.

But Quebec political tradition does not allow for putting things in perspective, for taking minor conflicts with a grain of salt, for distinguishing between a battle royal and a skirmish. Over five decades, Quebec has forged dogmas that no politician can ignore without fear of excommunication.

The weight of the years imposes a tradition, which is expressed in a martial vocabulary, full of superlatives — victories, retreats, penetrations, even extreme combat — that reinforce the sense of urgency and seriousness. It is a choke-hold that forces our leaders to choose the path of war, not because of the importance of the stakes, but because old battles are involved in which it is no longer possible to retreat.

Nationalism also finds expression in the pride we take in certain of its realizations. This is certainly progress. But pride, when expressed in a rigid context, can have perverse effects. Such is the case with the achievements of the Quiet Revolution, consecrated, defined as an integral part of the Quebec identity, and therefore untouchable. Pride, interpreted this way, instead of inspiring vitality and movement becomes, on the contrary, a justification for failure to act.

The result: Quebec is imprisoned in a political debate without issue between an undesired sovereignty and an impossible reform of federalism. This much we know. But that political impasse has given rise to other constraints. Those of a province that is more indebted, more taxed than the others and that offers fewer services. Those of a province that is poorer, but incapable of acquiring the tools that would secure it greater growth.

A Nationalism Unaware of Itself

Et voilà pour le nationalisme québécois. But can we find, in this Quebec experience, useful lessons for Canadian nationalism?

First, we have to ask ourselves whether Canadian nationalism really exists. The answer should be obvious, but it seems that many Canadians tend to negate its presence and are often unaware that certain of their attitudes, their gestures or their debates are expressions of such a nationalism.

Yes, Canadian nationalism exists. It rests on an obvious identity, rooted in an attachment to a territory Canadians have pioneered and whose integrity they do not wish to see threatened by a secession. It rests on a history, on political and social values, on a culture, on the coexistence of two official languages, on traditions, on lifestyles, on a vision of the role the country plays in the world, on institutions.

This sense of a nation runs through the entire spectrum of expressions: from the elite nationalism shaped by Pierre Trudeau's vision to the grassroots nationalism of Preston Manning, from the pride in the role played by Canada on the international stage to the wonderful "My name is Joe and I am Canadian." This cri de cœur, spontaneous and unsubsidized, has done more for the Canadian psyche than all of Sheila Copps's flags.

But Canadians are often unaware of the manifestations of their own nationalism. How many times has the constitutional crisis been presented as the result of pressures arising from Quebec nationalism — that eternal troublemaker — rather than as a confrontation of two nationalisms, whose visions are different and sometimes incompatible?

When we examine the conflicts that have brought Quebec and Canada into opposition, and in particular the last conflict, Meech Lake, it becomes plain that the seriousness of the crisis can be explained only by the fact that the Quebec demands, in a remarkable mirror effect, met up with an obstinacy every bit as symbolic and every bit as irrational on the other side.

Meech was the confrontation of identity myths in their purest form, where Quebec turned its demands into a life-or-death issue, but where Canada was ready to be torn apart, ready to risk breaking up rather than recognize a difference that would call into question its own vision of the country, including the completely absurd cult of the strict equality of the ten provinces.

The denial of Canadian nationalism can be found as well in those attempts to grade nationalisms — to define some variants as more noble than others, to oppose Canada's civic nationalism to Quebec's ethnic one. The question is not to determine who has the better nationalism — a childish sort of exercise — but to note that whenever it ennobles its own nationalism, a society will have a tendency to turn a blind eye to the more undesirable manifestations of it, and to disengage itself from its obligations to be vigilant.

The reality is more complex. Canada's nationalisms are hybrid phenomena. The Canadian variety has its origins in an ethnic nationalism, essentially British, which to be sure has undergone alterations with the intermixing of populations but which, over the decades, has experienced spasms of exclusion. Quebec nationalism, on the other hand, much more ethnic when it reflected the struggle of French Canadians, has for a long time rested less on ethnic origins than on language and culture, and, to the degree that the population of Quebec is undergoing a transformation, it is itself evolving in the direction of a civic nationalism.

Their dynamics are clearly different and reflect different social realities, among them the fact that Quebec nationalism is that of a minority, one that rightly or wrongly feels itself under threat and so must exhibit a constant degree of tension in the face of the majority — but one that entertains no doubt as to its identity. Canadian nationalism does not undergo that constant pressure; however, it must take greater care in defining the parameters of an identity whose borders are less focused and more fragile, and that sometimes rests on a certain voluntarism.

Where the two come together in a remarkable way is that both of them are built on a culture of dominated peoples, Quebecers being losers and Canadians being underdogs. French speakers feel dominated by English Canada, and to a lesser extent by English-speaking North America. Canada, dominated by a British Empire from which it belatedly broke free, lives in constant fear of American domination, and in moments of crisis is quick to mobilize in the face of threats from French Quebec. In both cases, we're dealing with reactive nationalism, triggered by threats, real or imagined, insecurity and fears: fear of free trade, fear of Quebec, fear of English-language pressures, fear of disappearing. And fear, as we know, is a collective sentiment that rarely brings a people to progress.

These obvious similarities are in large measure explained by the fact that the two nations share centuries of interaction, and, though lacking a common history, they have a common past, as well as the common values of the country they've built.

And there are instances where the two nationalisms, antagonistic though they may be, evoke exactly the same symbols to establish identities they judge to be different: the social-security safety net, for example, which is essentially the same, and which Quebecers as much as

Canadians perceive as an integral element of their own identity.

But where Canadian nationalism differs markedly is in the fact that it has no guidelines. And the consequence of Canadians tending to be ignorant of the existence of their own nationalism, or not seeing its manifestations, is potentially costly. Nationalism, here as everywhere, has its dangers; it can lead to excess and loss of control. For nationalism to be a positive force, it needs managing.

In this respect, the situation is more worrying in Canada than in Quebec, because Canada has no failsafe mechanism.

Quebec is obviously not perfect: the national question has generated its share of excesses. But we have mechanisms to limit loss of control, because we've lived so long with this national debate that we're acutely aware of its dangers. And also because we are politically divided, which provides us with watchdogs: federalist Quebecers who keep a close eye on sovereigntist excesses; English Canadians, always extremely vigilant where Quebec is concerned; and even the self-discipline of principled or image-conscious sovereigntists. Thus, when Jacques Parizeau, on the evening of his referendum defeat, spoke of "l'argent et les votes ethniques," he survived in office for twenty-four hours.

These checks and balances do not exist in Canada, because English Canadians are not aware enough of their own nationalism and because they are not divided on the unity issue: everyone is federalist, almost everyone reacts badly to the prospect of Quebec's separation, everyone shares a love of the country. (A revealing semantic detail should be noticed. What in Quebec we call the national debate or the Canada-Quebec debate or the constitutional debate has been defined in English Canada as the Unity debate, a term that contains its own values from the get-go and provides a fine example of Newspeak, so that anyone not sharing the Canadian point of view stands, by definition, against unity.)

The result is that no mechanisms exist to control nationalist excess. Some examples?

In my arena, that of print journalism, because of the divisions within my readership it is impossible to present extreme positions. There is such an imposed self-discipline that there are no Quebec equivalents of Diane Francis. There's no one in Quebec in upper management at a respectable publication read by a sophisticated public, for example, vicious enough to call for the imprisonment of elected politicians.

But the most revealing example of the loss of control of Canadians over their nationalism is probably the partitionist movement that arose in western Quebec in the days that followed the referendum almost won by the sovereigntists, in which anglophone municipalities sought to remain within Canada in the event of Quebec's secession. The movement, fraught with emotion, was understandable at the human level and reflected the trauma of people whose lives had almost been turned upside down.

The experience of the past decade, which has given rise to the formation of many new states, has taught us that the partitionist model, wherein portions of a new state remain attached to the previous state, has been applied in only one country, the former Yugoslavia. And that paved the way for a monstrous dynamic. Canada is, of course, not Serbia. But it is clear that the temptation of partition, in the event of a Yes victory, would lead Canada to choose the most explosive model of secession management imaginable.

And yet, that model, which should have been condemned out of hand because of the spiral of violence it risks producing, incompatible with Canadian traditions, was actually encouraged by the Chrétien government. And why? Because that partitionist movement was useful at the political level, in that its underlying thesis, the non-integrity of Quebec territory, could be used as a means of undercutting the sovereigntist cause.

This, in my view, is the typical case of a nationalist deviation whereby a nation, feeling itself threatened, develops defence mechanisms that fall outside the bounds of acceptable behaviour.

The Ills of Canadian Nationalism

The purpose of these remarks is not to launch myself on an attack on Canadian nationalism, but rather to underscore the idea that Canadians must take great pains to reflect on their identity, to define it, to trace precisely the outline of their nationalism; that herein lies the subject of a necessary debate. This is all the more necessary in that Canadian nationalism, like its counterpart in Quebec, is founded on a certain number of myths.

Canadians, often unsure of themselves, have erected a monument that would both better define Canada and enhance their self-esteem. This was a noble and healthy process; it lay at the basis of the vision of a modern Canada so fully embodied in the person of Pierre Trudeau.

Of course, there are characteristics of the Canadian identity that are deeply rooted: a history relatively free of violence, for instance; a capacity for coexistence among different cultures. But the fact remains that the three elements that probably most accurately define the Canadian identity are not the products of spontaneous generation. They are the products of human intervention and are extremely recent creations. I refer here to the attachment to a form of justice concerned with rights that finds special expression in the Charter of Rights and Freedoms. To a respect for plurality and difference, including multiculturalism. And to the values of generosity and sharing that underlie the social-security safety net.

The Charter, so essential to Canadian identity, is less than twenty years old; the very idea of multiculturalism is thirty years old; the welfare state began to take shape fifty years ago.

We could, at first glance, see in all this a sign of modernity, the ability of a society to define new values. But what fascinates is the speed with which these new values became sacred cows, which, in my view, is a reflection of an insecurity so great that Canadians have been led to seek life preservers rather than development tools.

We find the same thing in Quebec, where here as well the sacred cows are remarkably young — should we be talking of sacred calves? The Révolution tranquille — the Quiet Revolution — is forty years old; Bill 101 is twenty-five; and "le modèle québécois" is no more than about thirty.

The most striking phenomenon is that of the Charter. However much the principles of justice that it embodies derive from Canadian values, the tool — a charter in the American style and foreign to our legal traditions — is itself very recent. But this document, whose implications we have not yet digested, has already been internalized as a central element in the Canadian identity, to the point that it is no longer possible to deviate from it. In this adoption, as sudden as it has been absolute, there is something suspect that leads us to wonder how it was possible to be Canadian a quarter century ago.

Even if Canada has always had a tradition of immigration, the idea of pluralism that Canada holds to was essentially reformulated when multiculturalism became a cardinal virtue some thirty years ago, partly in response to the two-nations thesis and to the rising sovereigntist tide.

We are, I believe, in the presence of a myth here. It is true that Canada is a land of diversity, a land where tolerance has successfully taken root. But when we look at Canada's recent history, and even harder at its older history, we quite quickly discover that Canadian society stands up rather badly to the shock of difference. Canada deals well with a mosaic society, especially because the great diversity of the sources of immigration has a way of minimizing any threat. But Canada reacts quite badly when that diversity oversteps the boundaries of folklore and threatens the dominant culture.

We've seen, in the case of Quebec, how difficult it is for English Canada to accept the principle that part of the population can be different, and to formally recognize it — something that constitutes the very essence of respect for diversity. We've seen it with the First Nations, with whom we're still painfully seeking a way of coexisting in difference. We're seeing it now with the populations of the western provinces, who try to assert themselves through values that diverge from dogmas established in central Canada.

The perception — a false one, in our view — that Canada has of its own tolerance is accompanied by another perception, equally erroneous, about the behaviours that accompany this openness. And it's the image of gentleness that has led Canada to think it can resolve its internal crises through love — what we might call a touchy-feely nationalism.

This was the approach that gave us the love-in in Montreal on October 27, 1995, a few days before the referendum, when Canadians came to tell Quebecers how much they loved them.

This was an event that left me deeply uncomfortable, first of all, for conceptual reasons. The general theme of love strikes me as an approach that, in terms of resolving conflicts among peoples, is naive and inappropriate. It's true that Canadians of all origins, unlike what we tend to find in other binational or multinational states, carry on cordial relationships at the individual level. Montreal has never been Belfast.

It's rare for nations or communities that coexist in a single country to love one another. On the contrary, the very existence of multinational societies is usually the consequence of turbulent histories during which cultures, languages, religions and values have come into conflict. Canada is no exception: we can't help seeing that the values, the demands, the political choices of some have a tendency to, at the very least, irritate the others.

And there's nothing especially troubling about this. Love is not a functional basis of operations. It's more of an immature response to a complex problem. Tensions in binational states are normal; the wisest path and the most effective approach consist in accepting those tensions and managing them, rather than denying their existence by means of amorous outbursts.

The Montreal love-in failed to impress me in tactical terms as well. What I saw was a purely narcissistic exercise.

English Canadians, arriving in groups, demonstrated with other English Canadians, also in groups, and then took off again by bus, by car or by plane without ever having met the object of their effusions. The true gesture of love would have consisted in saying to Quebecers, "We love you, we don't want to lose you, and here's what we would do so that you could stay" — just as (to revisit interpersonal relationship analogies) a spouse would to prevent a separation. But the message in fact sounded more like this: "Don't leave, because we love Canada the way it is." What Canadians loved, that day, was not French-speaking Quebecers, but themselves.

The third pillar of this new nationalism is, of course, the culture of solidarity that finds expression in the values of sharing, a progressive tax structure, equalization policies and, above all, a social-security safety net of the European type.

The trap does not lie in these admirable policies, but in what they've generated in the collective unconscious. They have served to shape the Canadian identity because they help distinguish Canada from its threatening neighbour.

The result is a Canadian identity that is extremely vulnerable, because the soul of the people comes to depend not on the citizens, not on values, but instead on government programs, on civil servants, on budgets. A budget crisis, or even relatively innocuous acts like closing a railroad link or shutting down a regional radio station, become nation-destroying gestures. There is the concomitant tendency towards a paralysis of choice and of decision-making processes, since every change risks being perceived as an attack on the identity.

This identity attachment, over the years, has crystallized around the health-care system, which has become the symbol par excellence of the Canadian soul, the purest expression of its difference measured against American values. This attachment enshrined itself in a Canadian law on health care that, in the early 1980s, laid out the conditions to which provincial health plans would have to submit. And thus it is that the symbol of identity boils down to a law with five conditions and one formula, almost a mantra: one-tier system.

Not only is this a dogmatic approach, but it removes us from the real world and delivers us to the land of myths. Partly because Canada, despite its attachment to the formula, has never had a truly one-tier system. But mostly because this way of organizing a health-care network exists nowhere else in the industrialized world. Every regime, including those of left-leaning countries in Europe, allows the private and the public to coexist; they accept that not all activities are provided free of charge; they accept that the state shares the management of the system with other partners. What are defined as illegal acts in Canada and perceived as morally reprehensible avenues are accepted in every country that believes in solidarity.

The absolutely surrealistic nature of the thing was made clear to me in all its splendour when the former health minister Allan Rock, with whom I had shared this observation, answered me that yes, there was in fact a nation whose system rested on the same principles as ours . . . Cuba. This was not, alas, meant as a joke.

Rigidities That Come with a Price

There's a price to be paid for these rigidities, which entail numerous perverse effects.

There is first of all the fact that they deprive us of the possibility of exploring other avenues of reform. This seems to me to be the case in health care, where the choke-hold that Canada has applied to itself will make the colossal undertaking of re-engineering the health-care system, restoring the quality of care and people's confidence, much more difficult.

Similarly, the ideological framework that the Canadian government has imposed on itself will make challenges more difficult to meet, among them the necessity of raising the standard of living of Canadians and of lessening the gap that is deepening dangerously between us and our neighbour.

Another perverse effect, a much more disquieting one, is the development in Canada of an ideological orthodoxy. In Quebec there are pressures that discourage intellectuals from straying from sovereigntist dogma and thus running the risk of exclusion and mistrust. I know something about this. The same process is at work in Canada, on another basis, that of the Canadian social model. It is difficult to be a true Canadian without espousing the centre-left values that underlie our welfare state.

The idea of then premier of Ontario Bob Rae, when during our great constitutional debates he sought to have social rights enshrined in the Charter, reflects this tendency. The idea was noble and generous. But it carried with it important secondary effects, centring on the fact that for all practical purposes, the elements of a political program whose values are not necessarily universal and certainly not shared by all Canadians would have been constitutionalized.

This homogeneous political vision can also lead to abuse. For example, a federal minister told me that another former premier of Ontario, Mike Harris, was "un-Canadian," which reminds us how easy it is for nationalism to lead to intolerance.

This ideological orthodoxy contributed considerably, in my opinion, to fostering the alienation of the west and the anger against central Canada that found expression in the Reform Party and the Canadian Alliance. In effect, Canadian citizens were deprived of their democratic right, that of being *on* the right, and of expressing, in the organization of their collective life, values that differ from those of the central government. Therein lies a certain democratic deficit.

I do not support the Alliance. But I defend the right to be different, and even the possibility that other roads are capable of enriching our collective experience. And above all, I defend the inalienable right of Canadians to be able to choose.

This leads to another perverse effect that is beginning to appear in the Canadian political landscape. The ideological corridor is narrow to the point where only one political party can still embody the untouchable and unassailable values that define Canada, and that is the Liberal Party of Canada. So much so that Canada is gradually making its way towards a new situation, that of a single-party parliamentary regime.

That is why I fear that Canada is not well prepared for the challenges that the future holds in store, and that its nationalism, and the way in which that nationalism shapes the Canadian identity, risks being an obstacle rather than a positive force for progress.

The Canadian search for identity has, for some decades, instead of liberating Canada and Canadians succeeded in placing us in chains. A questioning of certain myths that are suffocating Canada has therefore become necessary, in order that Canada embrace a nationalism that is positive and creative and that the country have at its disposal the tools it will need in the years that lie ahead.

This is a question that needs to be faced all the more urgently in light of the new types of challenge that Canada will confront, most especially the impact of globalization on economic activity, on the role of states, on the fate of peoples. These pressures, which may turn out to be enormous, will demand from societies like ours — if we wish to resist them and continue to be what we are — strong identities and a great ability to adapt. For the moment, we would have trouble exhibiting either one or the other.

One way of finding that flexibility and ridding ourselves of sacred cows is debate. Canadians reflect all too little, except in specialized circles, on their identity, on the expressions of their nationalism. Taking comfort from their dogma, rocked in the cradle of ideological orthodoxy, Canadians have lost the daring, iconoclastic approach of the man that still inspires them, Pierre Trudeau. A little more reason, a little more lucidity would not harm the Canadian debate.

Another liberating tool is regionalization. I have no wish to talk here about the decentralization of power, or of the workings of federalism — however much I happen to be a supporter of decentralization. I will talk about something deeper, a state of mind, a way of perceiving the Canadian dynamic whereby the regions can play a role as a setting for initiative and for identity definition.

In Canadian history, the initiatives of regions, the competition that takes place among them and imitation have been major factors in national progress. I know there are some who associate modernity with a stronger central role, capable of countering what they see as provincial deviancy. But the regions are a source of creativity and energy that a sclerotic centre with an aging leadership cannot ensure. These regional identities exist in Canada, they are rich, and they should not merely be encouraged but showcased. They should be perceived as

factors that enrich the national identity rather than pressures from outside that constitute a threat to it.

Betting on regions seems to me more the order of the
day as globalization comes to have a greater impact on
the architecture of states, creates networks that transcend
the traditional logic of borders and deprives people of
frames of reference to which they've grown accustomed.
These upheavals tend to lead citizens to reinforce their
sense of identity at the regional level. This phenomenon
of regional reinforcement, obvious in Europe, will take
shape in Canada as free trade imposes a north-south
logic. Canada is obviously not prepared to facilitate this
process.

To this may be added another pressure linked to globalization, less obvious, more distant, that could be char-
acterized as a long shot but that seems to me to be
important to prepare for. And that is the impact of
continentalization, which to this point in time has found
expression mostly at the economic level.

North America — and soon simply the Americas, with
the Free Trade Area of the Americas — lags behind Europe
in terms of political integration. But the fact remains that
Canadians, and the younger ones especially, will progres-
sively develop what can be called a continental awareness,
a certain sense of belonging, a modification of what is

their implicit space. The mobility of students, of researchers, of management, the growth of transnational Canadian firms, the circulation of ideas — all this will have the effect that a growing number of Canadians, while remaining Canadians, will be North Americans as well in certain areas of their lives. This can now, unfortunately, be seen in some aspects of cultural life, but in time it will certainly come to affect other components of everyday living.

A new reality will emerge from this process: double identity, the mere evocation of which is bound to produce a shudder in many Canadians. But if the state is complex, it can nonetheless be managed — as we are beginning to see in Europe, where Germans, French and Italians are learning to be European citizens as well. This is something that Quebecers are very familiar with, being Quebecers and Canadians at one and the same time. Someday it will be your turn.

It can work — on the condition, of course, that the national identity is firmly grounded to begin with.

I'm not a specialist on the Canadian question — I'm not even Canadian in the same way that you are, given this double identity of mine. And that could possibly lead me to a degree of oversimplification. But my impression, despite certain misgivings, is that the Canadian identity is strong, in lifestyle, in the attachment to institutions, in values, in behaviours, in certain components of cultural life — much more than Canadian leaders, heirs to and caretakers of cultural insecurity, seem to believe.

The finest example, once again, is that of health care. It is not Jean Chrétien or Joe Clark or Stockwell Day or Gilles Duceppe or Alexa McDonough who is the custodian of the system; rather, it is Canadians themselves, who, without their politicians, have expressed in a thousand ways their objection to seeing a regime of the American type installed in Canada.

The rigidity of Canadian nationalism and of its symbols can be explained in large part by that obligation felt by our elites to furnish a bulwark protecting the Canadian identity. But that identity is strong enough to express itself without the artificial protection that the central power deems it its obligation to supply.

That paternalistic approach can have the opposite effect. In desiring to protect Canadians from themselves, in imposing on Canadians crutches for which they have no need, in instilling in them a sense of insecurity unjustified by reality, the risk is rather that the country as a whole will be enfeebled.

This, in essence, is the message I delivered to my readers in Quebec one year ago. It's a message, I believe, that applies equally well to Canadians, almost word for word.

～ Conversation Two

RUDYARD GRIFFITHS: Each of you in your speeches put forward new ideas and new models. For you, Alain, it was a vision of decentralization. Georges, you were encouraging a kind of nation-to-nation dialogue. Your Excellency, you were talking about the need to go back to some of our founding principles and values and begin a large-scale reform of these increasingly bureaucratic and complex organizations, which aren't necessarily delivering on those original values and principles.

There are some interesting tensions between those three kinds of models of reform or change. Alain, could you start?

ALAIN DUBUC: They're not models!

RUDYARD GRIFFITHS: Okay.

ALAIN DUBUC: One of the things we did in Canada was attempt to invent models and then to force them into place. They did not always fit with what the reality was, and I think we still have an idea of Canada that doesn't always fit. When I was talking about this on television, I didn't see it as a model that you can force on people but as a trend, as a way that people feel in defining themselves and recognizing similarities in a group. People are more comfortable identifying with smaller entities. If there's a model we can think about, it is Europe, even if they have some problems. We are seeing situations there in which some people suffer a lot from this loss of control of their destiny, but other people discover that being what they are — people from southern France or northern Italy and at the same time part of a great whole — is, in many ways, a very different experience. So you're French, you're sovereign French and you're European —

RUDYARD GRIFFITHS: And you're Mediterranean.

ALAIN DUBUC: — and so there's a much greater goal than just what you're urging the country to achieve. It's a kind of decentralization, where you're living in a smaller community but you adhere to something that is much bigger, with values that can bring you to evolve and to do something greater. It's not a model, but I think that is what we'll see in Canada.

RUDYARD GRIFFITHS: It's a concept.

ALAIN DUBUC: A concept based on what I see happening as a journalist. I see it in Quebec and I see it in other parts of the country.

JOHN RALSTON SAUL: It goes back to that idea of being comfortable. People in Canada are very comfortable with the idea that they are more than one thing at once. They might be holding back in the sense of participation on one level, because they're dissatisfied in various ways, as Georges points out. That happens in other areas as well.

But they are comfortable with the idea that they can be several things at once. That is a form of decentralization. It's almost a psychic decentralization. This country has the flexibility inside it to readjust itself, and it does so constantly. It goes this way, it goes that way, you know. It does things that look impossible, and the day they are done they're no longer impossible. We have it in our minds that we don't have to be one thing.

At a time when, of the twenty-odd Western democracies, about eighteen of them are moving in the direction of the nineteenth-century Canadian model, it would be crazy for us to hold on desperately to an idea that we've never actually represented, which is an eighteenth-century monolithic model, just because we live next door to the one remaining country of all the democracies that still believes in that monolithic model. They are the exception to the rule. No one else actually believes in it. Europeans don't believe in it. Australians don't really believe in it. They are, in a way, like Canadians.

RUDYARD GRIFFITHS: Georges?

GEORGES ERASMUS: Well, it's really interesting to see our regional identities getting stronger. If you're from the Prairies, you know what you're going through now with the drought, and in fact people are leaving that part of Canada (apart from Alberta, of course). But I think the sense of community, if anything, is getting stronger out there. Obviously British Columbia has the strength to grow, but you know the sense of identity and community there is quite strong.

I went through the interesting experience recently of having to move back to Yellowknife and experience the North again more closely than I had in some time. I noticed the changes that have happened there, who's involved. The kind of strict separation of community between Aboriginal and non-Aboriginal in different levels of the community in the north has really changed. The vision of Nunavut being created and the west staying part of the Northwest Territories has created a really interesting personality.

I do a lot of travelling across the country. My wife comes from Newfoundland, so for close to thirty years I've been going back and forth to Newfoundland, and the sense of community there is just immense. It's the same with the Atlantic provinces. For somebody going there, it's like a different world, never mind just a different country. So this concept that you are talking about of people identifying with the different regions, holding different values and so forth, is very true. You can experience it, and what's interesting is that there are a lot of universal values that still tie us all together. To me, this is probably going to be the interesting thing about where we're going to go as Canadians in the future, and it will probably, if anything, make us stronger. It might give us the kind of strength to build something like a collective character.

JOHN RALSTON SAUL: Or perhaps we're not able to admit that we've done it.

GEORGES ERASMUS: Maybe that's all we're talking about.

JOHN RALSTON SAUL: When I travel across the country, I find that people are very comfortable with values that are reasonably shared. But a lot of the public discourse, the official public discourse, which runs right through the entire country — in universities, politics, bureaucracy, journalism, historians — makes it very difficult to believe that there's anything there. But when you actually go out and talk to people . . . , when I go to Lac St-Jean, Quebec, whose do I find that discourse resembles most? Well, probably people in northern Ontario or Cape Breton or maybe Yellowknife.

Montreal's discourse, well, whose does it resemble most? Perhaps Vancouver's. In some ways Vancouver's resembles Montreal's most. And you could do this all across the country. The patterns are not the patterns that we're officially presented with on a regular basis.

I think everybody in this room has a sense of the positives and the negatives of the experience that we've all had in this country over the centuries. The public discourse doesn't take that into account. I use the word *linear* too much, but the public discourse is very linear. It doesn't really talk about the shape of the whole or the context or the circular nature.

I'm thrilled when I hear that pretty soon the workforce in Saskatchewan is going to be 50 percent Aboriginal. In a sense it brings us back to where we started the experiment. But it also means that there's going to be a completely new input of ideas coming out of Saskatchewan, and probably Manitoba, which is going to be about what happens when you have a southern territory with a major Aboriginal voice in it. Suddenly you have to come to terms with the whole history of the country, not just the year you happen to be living in.

ALAIN DUBUC: If it happens, you rediscover the virtues and differences.

JOHN RALSTON SAUL: Yes.

ALAIN DUBUC: And I think that Quebec is probably responsible for that, because differences there were seen as a tool to foster the separatist program. The situation in Quebec created a discourse in the rest of Canada in which this premise had to be denied because it would be seen as a menace to the structure. So you see the difference as a menace, as a weakness, while Quebec sees it as something manageable and rich in potential.

GEORGES ERASMUS: The same idea holds true for Aboriginal people.

JOHN RALSTON SAUL: The concept of complexity is the strength in the country. The nineteenth-century idea is that you can deny the complexity and so create a monolithic view.

ALAIN DUBUC: And the other thing is that the differences are useful to create the necessary tension you need in society. Because when we scratch the surface, there is much similarity and commonality.

RUDYARD GRIFFITHS: But people do see big differences in these small differences, at least in our public discourse.

Our discourse is often very polarized, I would say, around Aboriginal issues. What forces are at play out there that are leading us away from an appreciation of the beauty of small differences to a kind of antagonism about small differences? Is it a democratic deficit?

JOHN RALSTON SAUL: Let's compare Canada with Europe. The big difference between us and Europe is that Europe has leapt ahead in continent-wide economic structures and political administration — that is, from the top down — but there's a vacuum when it comes to culture. People are inventing it. The southern French are inventing or reinventing a Mediterannean relationship with Barcelona and northern Italy. But actually little has been done on the broader cultural front, apart from one television channel and a few scholarships named after Erasmus. They still have an enormous way to go. Whereas we have a long experience of debating the cultural content and working with it.

I don't think one should be too worried about how noisy the debate is. This is a non-violent country that compensates, to some extent, for the absence of violence by debating in a very aggressive way. I believe that a lot of the adjectives and adverbs that we use take the place of the physical action you might find in countries where the language is more controlled. So when my European friends come here, they are horrified by our relatively violent public language. If that language were used where they come from, it would lead to action. And I explain that it is actually in place of the action. The reason that they talk so carefully is that they know that if they talk any louder, they might fall back into the pattern of killing millions of their fellow citizens, which they've done and continue to do. Think of Ireland, the Basques, Corsica and so on. It's a very different approach towards debate.

GEORGES ERASMUS: I think you're right. I had not thought about that point, but you're absolutely right. I think your point is very interesting because that's probably one way we're very different from Americans.

RUDYARD GRIFFITHS: So we're not as polite as we think we are?

JOHN RALSTON SAUL: Not in political debate. I'm always saying that we mustn't confuse social, middle-class politeness with the roughness of public debate. The roughness of public debate is very important in this country. It has to be rough to maintain that movement between the regions and the languages and the differences.

ALAIN DUBUC: You have different nations and you have tensions and you do have anger, and public discourse is a way of venting. This is why I am not afraid when I see tensions rise. It's part of the process. We have to let all these things out. You see it with the First Nations, too; they have to express their anger.

We have this myth about love. It's part of the way Canada seems to define its relationships among groups. We love each other and so when you see this tension growing people feel betrayed. But this is a naive view of the nature of the relationship — it is not helpful to couch things in terms of love and hate.

Georges Erasmus
∼ The Lafontaine-Baldwin Lecture 2002

The Fairmont Hotel Vancouver
Vancouver, British Columbia
Friday, March 8, 2002

Introduction

I am honoured by the invitation to contribute to the LaFontaine-Baldwin lecture series, imagining the kind of

Canada we want in the twenty-first century. And I welcome the opportunity to reflect with you on the issues that we need to address in order to realize that vision.

To paint a picture of the Canada that Aboriginal people envision, I need only turn to the ideals of a good life embedded in Aboriginal languages and traditional teachings. The Anishinabek seek the spiritual gift of *pimatziwin* — long life and well-being that enable a person to gain wisdom. The Cree of the northern prairies value *miyowicehtowin* — having good relations. The Iroquois Great Law sets out rules for maintaining peace, *Skennen kowa,* among peoples, going beyond resolving conflicts to actively caring for each other's welfare. Aboriginal peoples across Canada internationally speak of their relationship with the natural world and the responsibility of human beings to maintain balance in the natural order. Rituals in which we give something back in return for the gifts that we receive from Mother Earth reinforce that sense of responsibility.

I would guess that most Canadians subscribe to these same goals: long life, health and wisdom for self and family; a harmonious and cohesive society; peace among peoples of different origins and territories; and a sustainable relationship with the natural environment.

Canadians would probably also agree in principle with the traditional Aboriginal ethic that our actions today should not jeopardize the health, peace and well-being of generations yet unborn.

If there is such a convergence of basic values between Aboriginal and non-Aboriginal peoples, why is communication between us so difficult, so riddled with misunderstandings and tension?

There is a problem of language. A study done for the Royal Commission on Aboriginal Peoples examined over two hundred commission and task force reports issued between 1966 and 1991. The researchers pointed out that even when we used the same words, Aboriginal people and government representatives were often talking about different things. The research also traced remarkable consistency in the issues and positions that Aboriginal peoples were articulating over those twenty-five years. I will return again to the issue of historical continuity in Aboriginal peoples' priorities. I first want to focus on the nature of discourse between our cultures. By discourse, I mean the way we carry on conversations.

Intercultural discourse is carried on predominantly in English or French. Since this requires translation of concepts and experience, there is the normal problem of finding words in a second language that approximate the meaning we want to convey. But beyond that, the discourse has been framed in terms that are often fundamentally alien to the way we think about an issue. Take "land claims," for example. Elders in our nations find it strange that younger leaders launch "claims" to lands that have supported our peoples since time immemorial. "Comprehensive and specific claims" are the terms around which the government of Canada is prepared to engage in legalistic dialogue. Aboriginal peoples have had to work with the prescribed terms in order to get land questions on the policy agenda, even though the language distorts our reality. The discourse is driven by an imbalance in power and considerations of strategy. In other areas as well — governance, health, education — Aboriginal peoples have been required to adopt language that is not quite our own.

I want to take most of this hour to suggest how dialogue with Aboriginal peoples might be framed in different terms, looking for language that expresses Aboriginal perspectives and also connects with the aspirations of a wide spectrum of Canadians.

Creating and sustaining a national community is an ongoing act of imagination, fuelled by stories of who we are. The narratives of how Canada came to be are only now beginning to acknowledge the fundamental contributions that Aboriginal peoples have made to the formation of Canada as we know it. We were major participants in the trade and commerce that supported settlement. We were partners in the treaty-making that opened access to lands and resources. We were in the front lines protecting Canadian borders in 1812–14. And we volunteered in extraordinary numbers in World War I and World War II to defend democratic values overseas. We are convinced that we also bring something of value as Aboriginal peoples to meeting the political and economic challenges that Canada faces in this new century.

If that contribution is to be fully realized, we need to engage in conversations that go beyond policy debates with governments. We need to talk "people to people" as well as "nation to nation."

I propose to try shifting the terms of discourse along three lines: from Aboriginal rights to relationship between peoples; from crying needs to vigorous capacity; from individual citizenship to nations within the nation state.

Aboriginal Rights: Relationship between Peoples

Aboriginal rights seriously entered the vocabulary of Canadian law and public policy in 1973, when a Supreme

Court judgment acknowledged that the Nisga'a of British Columbia had Aboriginal title to their traditional lands, based on their use and occupancy of those lands from time immemorial. The Nisga'a had never entered into treaties with the British colonial government or Canada. Members of the court were divided on whether enactments of federal and provincial law had extinguished Nisga'a title. Resolution of the Nisga'a land question would not be achieved until the signing of a treaty in 1998.

Aboriginal and treaty rights gained protection in the Canadian Constitution of 1982 with the provision that "the existing aboriginal and treaty rights of the aboriginal peoples of Canada are hereby recognized and affirmed." A series of Supreme Court decisions has given some definition of how these rights are to be interpreted under Canadian law, but there has never been a negotiated agreement between Aboriginal nations and Canada on the nature of these rights. Each court decision addresses a portion of the larger issue, raising a host of new questions. The Marshall decision of 1999 affirming Mi'kmaq rights, under a 1760 treaty, to earn a moderate living from the Atlantic fishery did not put an end to disputes about how resources are to be shared.

Gaining recognition of Aboriginal rights in the courts and entrenchment in the Constitution have been critical

to restoring Aboriginal peoples as active agents in direct-
ing our collective lives. Where land claims settlements
have proceeded, they have opened possibilities for social,
cultural, political and economic renewal. But there have
been some unfortunate side effects of the rights agenda.
An American Indian law professor has written that "like
other minority groups in our society, tribal Indians must
demonstrate a convergence of their interests with dominant group interests in promoting their rights." This is
difficult because "the rights they claim seem so alien and
opposed to the dominant society's legal, political, and
cultural traditions."

Aboriginal rights have been delineated in the context
of long, contentious court cases in which Aboriginal
interests have been pitted against Canadian state parties
who are purportedly representing the public interest.
Legal scholars and constitutional experts, standing
within the Canadian legal system, interpret what
Aboriginal peoples want and what obligations rest with
Canadian governments to accede to those claims.

Litigation is no way to build a community! It is not
the way preferred by Aboriginal peoples. We have a
history of treaty-making that stretches back long before
Columbus. Drawing on those traditions, through two
centuries of expanding settlement, the Mi'kmaq,

Mohawk, Ojibwa, Saulteaux, Cree, Dene and other Aboriginal nations sat down in councils and entered treaty negotiations to discuss how to establish good relations with newcomers. This is how Canada came to be a "peaceable kingdom," not one born of violence and conquest. A non-Aboriginal scholar working with the royal commission, who had spent years of his life researching treaty history, declared, "These are my treaties too. They legitimize my place in this land."

Aboriginal treaties are often described in legal terms as creating a *trust relationship,* one that invests the trustee with superior power and greater ethical responsibilities. For Aboriginal peoples, treaties created a *relationship of mutual trust* that was sacred and enduring. The bond created was like that of brothers who might have different gifts and follow different paths, but who could be counted on to render assistance to one another in times of need.

Renewing the relationship between Aboriginal and non-Aboriginal peoples in Canada is the major theme of the 1996 *Report of the Royal Commission on Aboriginal Peoples.* The RCAP report presented a comprehensive set of recommendations to restore a relationship of mutual trust, starting with an acknowledgement of historic wrongs, a ceremonial commitment to renewing the relationship and the establishment of laws and institutions to ensure that commitments would be acted upon.

It is now more than five years since RCAP reported to the prime minister and the people of Canada. There is a consensus among Aboriginal peoples, scholars and activists that little has changed in the interim. Underlying tensions over lands and treaty rights continue to boil up into open conflict. Litigation on residential schools wends its slow and tortuous way through the courts, bringing satisfaction and closure to no one. The federal minister of Indian Affairs has unilaterally announced a timetable for consultations and revisions to the Indian Act, without regard to the advice of RCAP that Aboriginal consent is essential to a renewed relationship.

In the months following the armed confrontation between Mohawks and Canadian authorities at Oka, there was an urgent and audible demand from the Canadian public to repair the relationship that had gone visibly wrong. In the decade since Oka, that sense of urgency appears to have subsided. Polling data indicate that there is still public support for spending to resolve social problems and, to a lesser degree, support for self-government and the cultural survival of Aboriginal peoples. The framing of the questions solicits answers

that reinforce a sense of distance and reluctant obligation. Aboriginal peoples, guided by their traditions,
would pose other questions: In this situation, how can
we establish good relations? In the circle of our relations,
how do we maintain harmony and well-being?

We have not found a way to ignite the imagination of
contemporary Canadians with the possibilities represented in the Kaswentah, the wampum belt recording
eighteenth-century treaties between the Iroquois and the
colonists that has struck a responsive chord with other
Aboriginal nations. The Kaswentah shows the wake of
two vessels, a First Nations canoe and a European sailing
ship travelling together on the river of life. The peoples
represented retain their own identity and autonomy, but
they are linked to one another by principles of truth,
respect and friendship. The two-row wampum belt is
often read as a symbol of separateness. In fact, it symbol-
izes a strong, ethical relationship between peoples.

Aboriginal Needs, Aboriginal Capacity

Perhaps one of the impediments to the mutual relationship envisioned by Aboriginal peoples is the notion that
we are an exceptionally needy population. The picture of

needs blocks out a perception of Aboriginal capacity. I suspect that media images of gas-sniffing youth in Davis Inlet are etched in the memories of most adult Canadians. There are other Aboriginal communities where substance abuse and clusters of suicide and suicidal behaviour are at crisis proportions. But there is also evidence from many quarters that Aboriginal peoples are in the midst of a remarkable resurgence — in education, healing and community wellness, the arts and economic activity.

Considering the primary importance of children in Aboriginal cultures it is not surprising that education was one of the first sectors where Aboriginal nations and communities moved to reassert control over their lives. Many schools in First Nations communities are now administered locally, and where possible they incorporate Aboriginal languages and cultural content in the curriculum. More youth are staying in school to complete a high school diploma, though a gap still exists between graduation rates of Aboriginal and non-Aboriginal young people. Post-secondary enrolments of registered Indian students have held steady at around 22,500 nationally for the past five years. The most remarkable fact about this group of students is that the largest proportion of them (42 percent) is over thirty years of age. The pattern is that Aboriginal students leave school as youth and return as adults, often with family responsibilities, to complete academic and vocational credentials.

Re-entry into post-secondary education has become more attractive with the introduction of Native studies and Aboriginal-specific programs in colleges and universities across the country. Aboriginal faculty are establishing a growing presence as role models, mentors and instructors. Aboriginal colleges and institutes have also become major players in post-secondary education. A few, like Saskatchewan Indian Federated College and the Nicola Valley Institute of Technology in British Columbia, offer provincially recognized diploma and degree programs. Most of the forty-three Aboriginal institutes across Canada have partnership arrangements with accredited provincial colleges and universities. The institutes, under Aboriginal control, are helping to narrow the gap in educational attainment by developing and delivering community-based, culturally relevant programs, serving adult students as well as youth.

Aboriginal initiatives in healing and wellness, like those in education, are showing high levels of effectiveness. Research is confirming that Aboriginal services are also cost-efficient.

Community Holistic Circle Healing was initiated in Hollow Water, Manitoba, in response to alarming incidents of sexual abuse, including abuse of children. Berma Bushie, one of the key participants in the strategy, described the situation facing the community in 1987: "The child welfare and legal system were at our door. The community had no involvement. Offenders were sent to jail where they had to deny their offence to survive, and two or three years later they were turned back into the community to offend again."

The thirteen-step program of intervention pioneered at Hollow Water engages the whole community, along with victims of abuse, offenders and their families, in assuming responsibility for restoring safety, health and balance.

In 2001 the ministry of the Solicitor General for Canada and the Aboriginal Healing Foundation sponsored a cost-benefit analysis of ten years' experience with Community Holistic Circle Healing. Over a ten-year period, federal and provincial ministries contributed $2.4 million to the project. A total of 107 offenders who acknowledged their offences were dealt with. The research calculated that for each two dollars of investment by federal and provincial ministries, the return was between six and sixteen dollars in services rendered in lieu of pre-incarceration, prison, probation and parole. These figures reflect the efficiencies achieved through community-led services that would otherwise have been provided by government agencies. The analysis does not take into account that the rate of reoffending over the ten-year period was less than 2 percent for offenders in Circle Healing, while estimated rates of recidivism are 13 percent for sex offences and 36 percent for other offences. Neither does this very conservative cost analysis account for benefits to the community that include improvements reported in child health, better parenting skills, increased safety and community responsibility overall. As a footnote, although residential school experience and its intergenerational effects are significantly implicated in the offences treated by Circle Healing, not one legal action had been filed by a Hollow Water community member as a result of residential school abuse.

Evidence is accumulating that Aboriginal organizations are very effective in mobilizing human resources to meet challenges. The Aboriginal Healing Foundation was established in 1998 to distribute $350 million allocated by the federal government to address the effects of physical and sexual abuse in residential schools. Many Aboriginal people who attended residential schools, or whose parents attended residential schools, experience post-traumatic stress, suicide attempts and life-threatening addictions, among other expressions of need. The Foundation has committed and distributed $156 million to community-based healing in the form of eight hundred grants. In June 2001 an interim evaluation surveyed just over three hundred of the projects funded to date. The survey found that 1,686 communities and communities of interest were being served; just under fifty-nine thousand Aboriginal people were engaged in healing projects, less than 1 percent of whom had been involved in healing previously; and almost eleven thousand Aboriginal people were receiving training as a result of funded projects. In an average month, thirteen thousand hours of volunteer service in the community were logged. Program investments are having a multiplier effect unheard of in government services.

Right across Canada, alternative justice projects, healing circles and Aboriginal agencies are reaching out and drawing angry, alienated, despairing individuals back into the circle of the community, where they discover their worth as human beings, recognize their relationships and begin to make their unique contribution to community well-being.

Aboriginal arts and artists are playing an important part in the revitalization of the Aboriginal community.

They are also making their mark in society at large. Aboriginal superstars have been around for a long time: Buffy Sainte-Marie and her presence at the Academy Awards and on *Sesame Street;* Bill Reid bringing Haida art forms to national prominence; Douglas Cardinal as the architect of the Museum of Civilization. We now have another generation of artists and writers giving expression to their Aboriginal identity and experience with eloquence and humour: Eden Robinson, a Haisla author, was nominated last year for both the Giller Prize and the Governor General's Award for fiction for her first novel, *Monkey Beach;* Tomson Highway has received international recognition as an author and playwright; Drew Hayden Taylor writes television scripts as well as plays and humorous columns. When Aboriginal people, especially youth, see Susan Aglukark on the music charts and Graham Greene in the movies, the range of scripts for their own lives is expanded. It was cause for celebration in February this year when an Inuit film, *Atanarjuat (The Fast Runner),* swept the Genie Awards, winning a total of six categories, including Best Picture, Best Direction and Best Screenplay.

The Aboriginal Peoples' Television Network, which began broadcasting in 1999, represents a huge step forward in Aboriginal arts and communications. APTN grew out of regional Aboriginal broadcasting initiatives, particularly the Inuit Broadcasting Corporation and Northern Native Broadcasting Network. It provides multiple lenses through which Aboriginal people can see the world and themselves and by which the public at large can view public affairs, community activities and cultural programming through Aboriginal eyes. APTN's influence is being extended as it partners with other agencies to produce and distribute a variety of programs, which, in turn, are broadcast on regional outlets.

I have mentioned that land claims settlements have opened economic opportunities for some Aboriginal communities. Development projects funded through government programs or private-sector partnerships are having an impact on others. I want to highlight the activity of Aboriginal entrepreneurs as another expression of Aboriginal capacity.

A 1996 survey by Statistics Canada identified over twenty thousand Aboriginal-owned businesses. This represents a threefold increase between 1981 and 1996. Forty-six percent of these businesses have at least one additional full-time, permanent employee. The numbers of Aboriginal women and Metis owners are showing the fastest growth. Businesses are concentrated in the primary sectors of fishing, trapping and farming, along with the contracting trades, but Aboriginal owners are also represented in a wide variety of enterprises, including management consulting, software design, manufacturing and tourism. These figures on entrepreneurship do not include community-owned businesses, which typically operate on a larger scale and set goals to promote training, employment and community economic development along with profit-making. Meadow Lake Tribal Council Forest Industries is a highly successful enterprise in the resource sector. Air Creebec and First Air, started with capital from claims settlements, are thriving in the highly competitive airline industry.

Despite the resurgence in Aboriginal capacity in the past thirty years, the gap between Aboriginal and general Canadian life opportunities remains disturbingly wide. While Canada regularly ranks first on the United Nations index for quality of life, registered Indians living on-reserve would rank sixty-third and registered Indians on- and off-reserve would rank forty-seventh after applying the UN criteria of education, income and life expectancy. Young Aboriginals are especially vulnerable. They are less likely than mature adults to have attained academic and vocational credentials, and they are hit hardest by unemployment. Moving from a reserve or rural settlement to the city improves income and employment prospects, but only marginally.

Strategies for building on Aboriginal capacity have been set out in the RCAP report and in subsequent forums. They include supporting community-led initiatives that mobilize Aboriginal people in diverse situations to deal with their own issues; creating space for Aboriginal institutions that provide sustained, effective leadership in accord with the culture of the community; promoting partnerships and collaboration among Aboriginal people, the private sector and public institutions to break down isolation and barriers to productive relationships; and recognizing the authority of Aboriginal nations to negotiate the continuing place of Aboriginal peoples in Canadian society, whether on their traditional lands or in the city.

Citizenship as Individuals: Nations within the Nation State

For most of the years since the first Indian Act was passed in 1876, being Aboriginal or "Indian" was perceived to be incompatible with being a Canadian citizen. When the option of enfranchisement, trading Indian status for voting rights, failed to attract individuals, more coercive measures were enacted, enfranchising Indians if they lived away from their reserves, joined the military, obtained higher education or, in the case of women, if they married a non-Indian. The object of policy, baldly stated in 1920 by Duncan Campbell Scott, superintendent of Indian Affairs, was "to continue until there is not a single Indian in Canada that has not been absorbed into the body politic and there is no Indian question and no Indian Department." The same object was reflected in the 1969 White Paper, which proposed, in the language of democracy, to make Indians "citizens like any other." The response of Aboriginal peoples to all these attempts to "break them into pieces" has been consistent resistance. Aboriginal proposals for a nation-to-nation relationship have proven problematic in attempted dialogue with governments and with Canadians at large. I want to spend a few minutes reframing the discourse on nation identities.

My first point is that Aboriginal peoples have maintained our identities as nations since time immemorial. As nations we made treaties with one another, with European emissaries and the Crown in right of Canada. As nations we have successfully asserted our rights before Canadian courts to enjoy benefits from our traditional lands. In negotiations leading to the failed Charlottetown

Accord on the Constitution, we won reluctant acknowledgement from Canadian governments that Aboriginal
self-government is an inherent right, not a privilege
granted by other authority.

It seems to us that the continuing existence of
Aboriginal nations is a political and legal reality as well as
a historical fact. How that reality is accommodated in
relations with the Canadian state and Canadian people is
a matter for negotiation. I would simply say to you that
we can't begin a dialogue on building a future together if
the conversation starts with the unilateral declaration
"You are not who you say you are!"

My second point is that most of the thorny issues
raised as impediments to nation-to-nation relations have
been confronted and resolved in the treaty concluded in
1998 by the Nisga'a Nation, Canada and British
Columbia. The treaty secures to the Nisga'a control of a
portion of their traditional territory and a share of
natural resources in other areas. It frees up vast areas of
Nisga'a homelands for use and development by Canada,
British Columbia and commercial interests. The treaty
deals with Nisga'a legislative powers, government-to-
government fiscal transfers and taxation.

I'm not proposing that the Nisga'a treaty should be a
template for nation-to-nation relations, but it does

provide an example of how a practical agreement can be put in place without undermining the integrity of the Canadian federation.

My final point on nation-to-nation relations concerns the practical benefits to Aboriginal peoples and to Canada of recognizing and accommodating the authority of Aboriginal nations. Stable Aboriginal governments with recognized jurisdiction, resources to implement decisions and legitimacy in the eyes of citizens can achieve social and economic renewal more effectively than federal and provincial governments have been able to do. The evidence is in.

The Harvard Project on American Indian Economic Development reported in 1992 on research in fifty ventures over a five-year period. The project attempted to determine why economic ventures in some tribes succeed and in others fail. The findings, confirmed in subsequent studies, showed that effective governance is a critical factor in fostering economic development. The characteristics of effective government were identified as 1) having power to make decisions about a community's own future; 2) exercising power through effective institutions; and 3) choosing economic policies and projects that fit with values and priorities, that is, the culture of the community.

The findings on economic development in American Indian tribes are mirrored in a World Bank study of 1998 that found a negative correlation between foreign aid and growth. The study raised doubts about the assumption that injections of capital from abroad would be the main way of achieving significant social and economic benefits in developing countries. Having effective government institutions at the community level that support sound economic policies and inclusive social policy is far more influential than previously understood.

Recognizing nations and establishing institutions to implement the inherent right of self-government are important, but they are not sufficient to enable Aboriginal people to thrive in Canada. The Royal Commission on Aboriginal Peoples pointed out that political gains will be hollow without the economic means to sustain them. The economic base for many Aboriginal nations is to be found in the potential for wealth standing on, lying under or flowing through their traditional territories.

The United Nations Human Rights Committee took up the theme of lands and resources in its 1999 review of Canada's compliance with the UN Covenant on Civil and Political Rights. The Committee challenged Canada in these words:

With reference to the conclusion by RCAP that without a greater share of lands and resources institutions of aboriginal self-government will fail, the Committee emphasizes that the right to self-determination requires, *inter alia,* that all peoples must be able to freely dispose of their natural wealth and resources and that they may not be deprived of their own means of subsistence. The Committee recommends that decisive and urgent action be taken towards the full implementation of the RCAP recommendations on land and resource allocation.

The Future Begins Now

As I was in the final stages of preparing this talk, I was anticipating the questions that might be stimulated by this vision of building a common future. Can we get there from here? What are the costs? Is it in the public interest of Canada as a whole?

At the same time, a historic event was taking place in northern Quebec. In February, the Grand Council of the Crees and Premier Bernard Landry signed a nation-to-nation agreement to guide development in the region

over the next fifty years. The agreement sets a new standard for securing the consent of an Aboriginal nation to
development on its lands. It provides for sharing of
resource revenue from three sectors: electricity, mining
and forestry; and it recognizes the Cree people's right to
determine their own economic future.

Grand Chief Ted Moses, in his speech at the signing
ceremony, answered many of the questions I was thinking about. He said, in part:

> For twenty-six years the Cree Nation has been
> fighting to breathe life and spirit into [the James
> Bay and Northern Quebec Agreement] that has
> become the subject of many legal challenges —
> challenges from the Crees, challenges from the
> governments and from others.
>
> Today we will be able to put that adversity
> behind us, and redirect our attention, our energy,
> and our imaginations to our common effort, in
> real partnership with Quebec, to plan for a future
> that includes Les Québécois, includes the Cree
> People. . . . The agreement we are signing here
> today . . . is the first serious step in the implemen-
> tation of the recommendations of the Royal
> Commission on Aboriginal Peoples, and is, for now,

the *only* instance in Canada of a governmental authority recognizing and implementing the operational principles of self-determination called for by the United Nations Human Rights Committee.

I have argued that a new relationship between Aboriginal peoples and others in Canada is urgently needed, that it will bring benefit to both Aboriginal and non-Aboriginal partners, that it is consistent with Canadian law and social values.

There is another compelling reason to join our efforts to achieve good relations. The world needs a model of peace and friendship between peoples that Canada is uniquely positioned to provide.

The greatest challenge to the world community in this century is how to promote harmonious relations among peoples of disparate origins, histories, languages and religions who find themselves intermingled in a single state. The U.S.S.R. has fractured into constituent nations. The former Yugoslavia has fallen into bitter strife along nationalist and religious lines. The troubles in Northern Ireland continue to flare up in spite of international efforts to broker peace.

Canada and Canadians have played a prominent and distinguished role in advancing the philosophy, practice and protection of human rights around the world. Michael Ignatieff, in a recent book, cites Canada's remarkable inventiveness in finding ways to enable a large, multi-ethnic, multinational state to survive and even prosper. Negotiation and compromise were instituted as civic values in the historic alliance of anglophones and francophones led by Baldwin and LaFontaine in 1848. But before that, Aboriginal peoples had introduced warring Europeans to the protocols by which nations could relate to one another as brothers, travelling the river of life sharing prosperity and hardship, autonomous enough to guide their own vessels but close enough to render mutual aid.

Public discourse on relations with Aboriginal peoples has been overtaken by inertia in recent years. The issues that flare up periodically within Canada and mar Canada's reputation as a human rights advocate internationally will not disappear on their own. The words of Zebedee Nungak, an Inuit leader, speaking in the final moments of a First Ministers' meeting in 1987, ring true for many Aboriginal people today:

> We continue to have a hope that this great country, which we embrace as our own, will have the sense and the decency — not that I doubt its

decency — to someday, in my generation, recognize our rights, and complete the circle of Confederation, because if it is not going to be done in my generation, I have my son standing behind me who will take up the fight with your sons and your sons' sons.

The costs of conflict, in the courts and in society, are unsupportable. The costs of doing nothing escalate with each generation. We have the capacity to imagine a better future and we have the tools at hand to realize it. Let us decide now to pursue our common goals together, to achieve long life, health and wisdom for all, good relations and peace among peoples and respect for the earth that supports us.

Masi cho. Thank you for your attention.

～ Conversation Three

RUDYARD GRIFFITHS: Is there a new way of listening to each other in this country? Is there something that Aboriginal people in particular are very good at, that could inform the way we listen to each other? Might it actually change the debate if we listened to each other in a different way?

GEORGES ERASMUS: Well, as I tried to suggest in the presentation I made, yes, it would obviously be better, because we would approach things from a different angle. We would try to look at how relations would be improved if we actually tried to regard the interests of everyone as equally important. But the reality is that we have structured the way things happen at the moment around government, and Aboriginal people and the rest of Canada are not involved. Unless Canadians really do get involved, I don't see things changing quickly.

There's a comment I wanted to make earlier about values and participation and so forth in the context of the discussion about NGOs. I wanted to tell you that, previously, Aboriginal people actually had more power in this country. In the past couple of decades, there was a huge coalition created across the country — church groups, labour organizations, university organizations, women's organizations and so forth — to lobby in support of very clear positions that average people have. It allowed a number of things to take place, and one was the postponement of the Mackenzie Valley pipeline. It took a lot of work to include Canadians, and we created organizations to work with southern communities. It made a big difference. Now that it's no longer there, you really can feel it. For instance, the funding for the Assembly of First Nations was cut in half, for whatever reason, just at the whim of the minister of Indian Affairs.

Virtually nothing happens now. Whereas, while we were at the height of this coalition we created, that would not have happened.

JOHN RALSTON SAUL: I think the difficulty is that you can build coalitions outside, and they're very often essential. In fact, that's usually the way public policy reforms start. But historically what tends to happen, not just in Canada, is that in order for them to succeed in the long term, they become part of the inside debate, and they thereby take the argument of the coalition from the outside to the inside. And of course, that requires certain compromises, and in a way everybody is somewhat unhappy. But on the other hand, that does carry it into the mainstream. The argument was perhaps that maybe it couldn't happen at that stage because there were too many problems.

GEORGES ERASMUS: I don't know that that can always be the case, and I don't know if that is the conclusion, because there are only so many members, there are only two or three hundred members of the coalition, and what about the thirty million of us who are living in the country? That leaves us out in the cold.

JOHN RALSTON SAUL: Not really, because at some point there has to be a critical mass of people inside — on the committees, in the party meetings, in the meetings with the deputy ministers — who are part of that representation debate. There has to be a critical mass. It's almost a matter of how many times people sitting in the chamber or around the chamber actually voice certain opinions. Think, for an example, of the environmental question. You see that the absence of a critical mass of serious environmentalists inside is perhaps what has held it back, in spite of the popularity of the movement in most Western countries. The issue just hasn't been transferred over into representative politics.

GEORGES ERASMUS: I'm not disagreeing with that notion. You have to have strong representatives inside, otherwise you're always outside. But what I'm thinking is left out is that democracy has evolved to be an election every four years. You're a member of a party, perhaps, and you write letters to your MP, they have maybe two public meetings a year, and that's about it. If you're somebody who wants to take part, that's your only opportunity. We're still a long way from having the kind of society in which people can really participate.

We spend a lot of time in the north considering how

we might create a society in the Dene area that actually reflects the values of the Dene. When we tried to do it, we found we needed more public participation. It wasn't possible for us just to create a society that redistributed our power among a few people and said, "Okay, you're the best among us, you govern," because it was so alien to the kind of values that we grew up with. We always maintained the right to participate, and we could exercise our right to have somebody to represent us, we could call them back if we didn't like what they were doing.

It's easier in a smaller society, and it gets more challenging with a bigger country and all the rest of it. But we're starting to get the means of communicating electronically and so forth, so it seems to me that we need to find ways to participate in this society a lot more than we do now.

ALAIN DUBUC: It works in small communities with small issues. People seem to participate in local politics, school boards, hospital boards because they are concerned. And it's the same in big cities. But when you're talking about NGOs and the mainstream, I think your question about how people don't listen to each other is truer with a majority. You usually don't listen to a minority. It's part of the normal life of a majority — not listening to and not taking into account the constraints that go with the dialogue. The only time you can engage the majority in dialogue is when you shout, when you make noise and annoy the majority and force it. And maybe it's the same way with some of the issues that are important within the majority. You have to force your issue or your cause to be taken into account. When it has no choice, the majority tends to listen, but the first reflex of the group is to deny problems or deny issues, because it takes them into account only when it is forced to. When you are first forced to look at the problem and then you see that you have a problem, this is when you change.

JOHN RALSTON SAUL: I think you're absolutely right about the question of participation, and I think probably all three of us agree that that is the biggest challenge. Reform has to end up in a place such as a parliament; otherwise, you're in a dangerous regime, which is direct democracy. We know that direct democracy can work in smaller communities and on smaller questions — not of smaller importance, but in numbers — because the people can actually either get together or almost get together. They can see how the participation plays out. The difficulty is that when we get to a million, seven million, thirty million, we really have to have a series of reverberations in order to get to what it is that we're going to do somewhere down the road.

We have done a lot throughout Western society, including Canada, over the past decade or so to discourage the idea that it would make a difference if you participated officially. People have become very discouraged about whether they can make a difference. All the assertions that there are great forces at work rolling over us makes people feel, "Well, why would I go to the local meeting if, after all, there are enormous economic forces at work that are taking my power away? Why should I bother?" I really think that the greatest labour that is there for those who believe in participation is to go out and relaunch, recreate, redefine the nature of participation for a citizen in a medium-sized democracy that has inside it all sorts of groups and minorities and languages and so on.

The other thing, at the centre of that argument, Alain, for me — and you'll say that this is a very anglophone argument, perhaps — is to really remind people, rather than convince, to remind people that the reality of Canada is that there is no majority and there never has been a majority. When one talks about the anglophones, for example, they were never one thing. They were always divided — either by their origins, going right back to the beginning with the Irish, the English, the Scots and the various other people who spoke English, or by religion or by region. They were never one group, and it was only very rarely in history, and usually at our worst moments, that somebody was able to assemble them as a majority, usually through anger, which is the worst kind of thing, and false love.

This has always been a country of minorities that at its best, or even at its medium-best, works most effectively as a country of minorities. And when you think about it that way, it makes you think about government differently, because suddenly you realize that the purpose of winning is to be able to deal with the multiplicity of minorities. Citizens are very comfortable with that idea. They're not really looking to be convinced that there is either a majority or a great majority.

Look at the relative success of developing stronger systems for French-immersion schooling, new rules for francophones outside of Quebec, and putting them in place both inside Quebec and outside of Quebec. That has a very interesting reverberation, I think, not simply for third languages such as Spanish or German or Chinese, but also for Aboriginal languages. Once you've shown, through systems such as those used for immersion

French and for francophone minorities outside of Quebec, that French can work, then suddenly you think, well, there are some interesting examples here of why it should not be so difficult for Aboriginal languages to take not a defensive position but an offensive position.

So once you start entering into the spirit of a country of minorities, it doesn't lock anyone out. It actually makes it possible to imagine the other options that might otherwise seem very, very difficult. You know, when you say to people in Toronto or Montreal or Vancouver that there are fifty Aboriginal languages and we're losing them, they don't know what to say. But when you say to them, "Look at what we did with French in various places — and besides, these languages are part of the multiplicity of your culture — do you want to really lose them? Do you want to lose access to that?" Then people say, "Well, we did it for this, we could do it for that."

RUDYARD GRIFFITHS: As a kind of a segue into a final phase for our discussion, could we have each one of you walk out on a proverbial plank and say where you see the potential for real reform and what shape that would take, if we were to re-imagine a new or democratic set of institutions and values, what would Canada be in fifty years?

ALAIN DUBUC: Fifty?

JOHN RALSTON SAUL: Not twenty-five, fifty? Where did this come from, this fifty?

RUDYARD GRIFFITHS: What would the country look like? Alain, in your case you talk about the North Americanization of Canada, and this may not actually be, for you, necessarily a bad thing, people thinking of themselves as part of a North American identity.

ALAIN DUBUC: I think that NAFTA — which was a business deal, a commercial deal, not a cultural deal at all — adds something wonderful. Mexico is now part of the picture, and it opened the minds of Canadians for the first time to a real foreign country. When you have trade negotiations with Americans, we are very integrated economies, so there was no real surprise in the fact that you could sell more into Maine or Iowa or Manitoba. But when you get Mexico in the picture, you begin to think in terms of another language, another culture and a society that is also a privileged one in some ways, and you have to think of your links to other parts of the world. We never did. Europeans did, and Americans did because they are a superpower.

RUDYARD GRIFFITHS: Are you saying there would be a fourth pillar in fifty years, adding Hispanic to English, French and Aboriginal ones?

ALAIN DUBUC: It's not the same. The language can be a tool to broaden our minds, but it will not become part of our culture. I do think, though, that we will begin to see the territory in a different way. Our conception of ourselves will not be the same either, so I think it will lead us to a much stronger identity than we have now. It will be the same for the Aboriginal peoples, because kids will go to the south and they will study and it will change their identity. It will be interesting.

But I'm not talking about reform, which was your question. It's about evolution. I'm not sure, because when we in Canada talk about reform, we talk about all kind of structures — how can we amend the definition? Maybe it will be very healthy for all of us for many decades not to think in those terms. And that is how you evolve. How you think differently is more important than what kind of reforms are occurring.

RUDYARD GRIFFITHS: So a discourse of values, not institutions.

ALAIN DUBUC: And cultures.

RUDYARD GRIFFITHS: Georges, how do you see the Canadian democracy in fifty years? What will it look like?

GEORGES ERASMUS: Well, we're probably going to be in a place where there's going to be a lot more land issues that have been resolved for Aboriginal people. The population is going to be interesting, because it's likely going to mean that in the Prairie provinces the workforce will be largely Aboriginal, and in the north also. So it's probably going to mean that the influence of Aboriginal culture is going to be stronger than it is now, because you're going to have a lot of people who have stopped being defensive and started to become creative. We will have been building for a long time, and you're going to have lots of places of strength in the Aboriginal community. You're probably going to see changes in medicine, for instance. Traditional Aboriginal practices in medicine will evolve in a way that brings together ideas that Western medicine has been working on for a long time and so forth.

You're going to see a very strong spiritual evolution. Christianity and its influence on Aboriginal people will not be as strong as it is at the moment because there's a rebirth happening in Aboriginal spirituality. You will probably still have a strong Christian influence, but what's going to be interesting is the rebirth — I didn't mention this in my speech, but it's quite immense, it's quite amazing what's happening in the Aboriginal spiritual beliefs.

So you probably will have strong Aboriginal languages, though you'll have lost a number. The ones that survive will be strong. And there will have been a pan-cultural process that has taken place because Aboriginals are looking everywhere for values, and it might not exactly be their own that they're looking for.

And then the other thing that's happening is that within a specific Aboriginal nation, there is growth happening there and knowledge emanating from it, so that we'll see both for a while. In the same way that Canadians share values, Aboriginal people are sharing as well. But within their own individual nations there has also been change happening. People are going back to, and understanding, what the original values were, and history and so forth.

I wouldn't be surprised if, at the national level, you have very strong Aboriginal politicians with more prominence than they now have, that are actually part of the centre.

RUDYARD GRIFFITHS: It would be part of the normalization of the Aboriginal role?

GEORGES ERASMUS: Yes, exactly.

RUDYARD GRIFFITHS: Finally, Your Excellency.

JOHN RALSTON SAUL: It seems to me that there are a
couple of things, and one is that if you were to believe
what is commonly said about the nation state today, this
discussion wouldn't need to take place. Theoretically,
nation states are becoming less and less powerful and less
and less meaningful. My gut feeling is that what we're
witnessing now — and I think it'll probably go on for at
least a decade and perhaps more, because usually waves
tend to be twenty or twenty-five years — what we're now
witnessing is the return of nationalism in the broadest
possible sense, simply because the movement for a
quarter of a century has been to drive everything on the
basis of economics and uncontrollable forces and that has
produced fear, anger, alienation among a lot of people.

You can like it, you can dislike it, you can attribute it
to many different things, but it's there, and you're starting to see the reactions everywhere. You're seeing a very
frightening return of false populism throughout Western

civilization, particularly in Europe, and a lot of things that ten years ago would have been considered impossible. Fascists in senior positions in government in Europe, once completely impossible, are now treated as normal in several places.

We were talking earlier about the body politic and how anger comes out. Well, you can see this wave of returning nationalism. Now, nationalism can be many different things. There are two implications to take out of this: one is that the nation state isn't finished; probably the nation state is not in the process of disappearing. And we are going to be faced, as everybody else is, with the question of what this means: is it going to result in what I call negative nationalism, or in positive nationalism or some variety of the two? Most of this conversation, I think, has been about the possibilities for positive nationalism.

You haven't heard a word here from the three of us touting the virtues of anything that would be traditionally called nineteenth-century nationalism, which I think we could call more or less negative. But that nineteenth-century nationalism is coming back all through the West.

And so part of the dialogue is trying to figure out how you give form to the positive aspects of it. What this country might look like in fifty years will be dependent to a great extent on whether we're able to give this value a shape. I think one of the key factors here is a particularity of Canada, which is this: no matter how much our population grows, it's going to be minute in comparison with our land; therefore, unlike Europe and the United States, and like Australia and a few other places, no matter how many people live in the cities, we have to maintain the tension between the place and the people. If we fall too much into the universalization of political science and economic theories about how a country works, we'll find ourselves attempting to apply theory systems and models that make sense in the United States and Europe but actually would be totally destructive for living here. And as the cities get bigger and bigger, they have a tendency to turn in on themselves — perfectly understandable. One can sympathize. You know, all three of us either are from or have lived in those cities. They have problems. But if they turn in on themselves, they turn their backs on the *place,* and that will simply accentuate the problems of both the country and the cities.

I think we have to come back to the question of participation that was raised earlier. If we can actually figure out ways for people to participate, that will take us down the road to positive nationalism, to the country working as an interesting experiment. And we have to keep thinking of it as an experiment. It will continue to be a place of minorities, and I think that the places from which the new ideas are going to come in the next fifteen to twenty years are probably not going to be Ontario and Quebec. I think they are going to come from Aboriginals, because of all the things that have been said: the critical mass is changing in the Prairie provinces, the north and so on. And besides, that's where there's the biggest change happening. Where the biggest change is happening is where the new ideas come from. We've got to open our minds to those ideas, and we have to stop being obsessed by what's still wrong in those communities and start saying, "Well, what's interesting that's happening?"

I think British Columbia is also going to have an enormous role to play. It's a bouillon of ideas at the moment. For example, to a great extent, environmentalism came out of British Columbia, and it may find a form that will change the face of the country. I hear arguments in Vancouver that, when you sit back and look at them from a distance, could be on the positive side, demonstrating the new impetus. And then I think, interestingly enough, that the Maritimes — which hasn't had a chance to bring a lot to the table for quite a while — did, in the nineteenth century, bring an enormous amount: the first democratic government, Joseph Howe, public education. I think the Maritimes are coming around an interesting corner, which is a combination of crisis and new ideas at the same time, and that the Maritimes may have something new to bring. I'm not quite sure what yet, but whenever I'm there, I sense something is happening, just underneath, coming up.

And then the final thing is — and this is almost administrative philosophy, what I talked about a bit in my speech three years ago — we have very successfully built up a whole range of public services in this country. Because we do it in an ad hoc manner, it becomes like an opaque mountain, and there's been a false debate about whether those services work. All that's wrong with most of them is that they are built up in the opaque stage, and that from time to time you have to clarify the purpose, the original and continuing purpose. It's a really, really boring process. It's law reform, really boring stuff, administrative reform, clarification. But if you don't actually deal with it, you can become a victim of the opaqueness. Then you end up thinking that the structure is more important than the intent. We have to get back to the intent of those policies and how they relate to the values that might be shared across the country.

ALAIN DUBUC: I have one more thing to say. The issue also has an impact on the way that we see this place and the necessity of this place. When we talk about the gap between public life and the needs of people, there's a certain relevance to government. The case then may be that some of the participation that we lost in the past twenty-five years can be recovered. I think it's possible because we will need to protect ourselves and to define ourselves, and globalization, of course. I totally agree with the concept of positive nationalism and in Canada we have an advantage that some European countries don't have: we have three kinds of nationalism in the same country. That can be dangerous, because they feed on each other, but the fact that we have three courses may provide a protection against the great danger of nationalism.

JOHN RALSTON SAUL: Related to that is the question, From where do we draw our new ideas? Some from inside Canada. But where do the ideas come from outside of Canada? I think it's problematic, and it's a return to the nineteenth-century colonial mind, to think that we have to draw from our closest neighbour. More and more we send our kids there for a brilliant education, but it's an education designed to run the most amazing and powerful empire in the history of the world. It isn't very helpful in training for people coming back to a country of thirty million who already think of themselves as minorities.

A concentrated effort needs to be made to create possibilities for Canadians to be educated abroad, post-graduate or whatever, but off the continent. I'm talking about thousands of kids going to Australia, going to Italy, going to Chile, going to Japan, going to Scandinavia. This has to happen if we're going to bring in ideas from outside, from places, from situations that resemble ours. I'm sure there are dozens and dozens of what I would call nuts-and-bolts things we could be doing that would change the pieces, the cards we can play with inside the country, the potential. Some of that's been happening among Aboriginals, Aboriginals moving around the world quite a bit, talking with other Aboriginal groups. New Zealand, for example, has had quite an impact, I think, in terms of shared ideas, no?

GEORGES ERASMUS: Yes, in fact one kind of globalization is definitely happening among Aboriginal people. It is the sharing of ideas and strengths, and it's something that I think is only beginning, because there's so much to share. And when you share when you're weak, you're actually strengthening again, and you build a community that you can provide for.